The Fragile Earth Navigating the Global Environmental Crisis

Mohsin Siddiqi

Copyright © [2023]

Title: The Fragile Earth Navigating the Global Environmental Crisis

Author's: John Anderson

All rights reserved. No part of this publication may be reproduced, stored in a retrieval system, or transmitted in any form or by any means, electronic, mechanical, photocopying, recording, or otherwise, without the prior written permission of the publisher or author, except in the case of brief quotations embodied in critical reviews and certain other noncommercial uses permitted by copyright law.
This book was printed and published by

ISBN:

For permission to reproduce any of the material in this book.

Table of content

Chapter name   **Page No**

Chapter	Page
1. Problems Facing the Environment, in Brief	1
2. The Consequences of Climate Change	10
3. We are losing biodiversity and ecosystems.	20
4. Environmental Hazards and Human Health	30
5. Scarcity of resources as a result of excessive use	40
6. Aspects of Society and the Economy	50
7. Administration and Control	61
8. New Green Technologies and Methods	72
9. The Role of the Individual and the Group	83
10. Prospects for LongTerm Sustainability	94
11. The Need for Rapid Alteration	104

Chapter 1.
Problems Facing the Environment, in Brief

1.1- Introduction to the global environmental crisis.

Introduction: Making Sense of Our Worldwide Environmental Crisis

Our earth is in the midst of a truly unprecedented environmental crisis in the 21st century. The Earth's formerly thriving biosphere today shows the wear and tear of constant human interference. The looming dangers of climate change, biodiversity loss, pollution, and resource depletion make this catastrophe the defining task of our era. In an effort to educate and encourage readers to become stewards of our world, "The Fragile Earth: Navigating the Global Environmental Crisis" goes deep into the heart of this critical and complex subject.

Our tale opens with a salute to the incredible past of our planet. The planet's ecosystems have developed and flourished for billions of years thanks to a careful balancing act. Species, ecosystems, and the availability of essential materials all form interdependent parts of Earth's living fabric. But as the human population grows and industrialization spreads, we have increasingly upset this equilibrium, setting in motion a series of environmental crises that endanger the security of our planet.

Climate change is a major issue that needs immediate attention. Greenhouse gases like carbon dioxide and methane have been released into the atmosphere in large quantities due to human activities including the burning of fossil fuels, the clearing of forests, and various industrial processes. These gases act as insulators, driving a rapid increase in global temperatures. More frequent and intense heatwaves, droughts, floods, and other extreme weather events are already a result. Populations and economies in low lying coastal areas are being threatened by rising sea levels.

The effects of climate change are farreaching and permeate every level of our communities, not just the environment. Climate change poses a danger to food and water security because it affects agricultural production and freshwater supplies. The expenditures of disaster response and recovery put a pressure on economies. Communities already struggling to make ends meet are hit especially hard. Recognising that climate change is not some faroff danger but rather a present one that affects everyone is crucial in light of the rising situation.

The loss of biodiversity is a major contributor to the world's current environmental predicament. At an alarming rate, species are disappearing from Earth's ecosystems. This destruction not only lessens the planet's natural splendour but also undermines its ability to sustain life. Biodiversity helps ecosystems remain stable, protects against climate change, and guarantees access to vital resources. However, many species are on the verge of extinction due to habitat destruction, pollution, overexploitation, and invasive species. Human health, economics, and cultural legacy are all at risk as a result of biodiversity loss, which has farreaching effects beyond the natural world.

Another widespread problem is pollution. Toxic chemicals are polluting our environment at an alarming rate. Pollutants released from factories, farms, and cities are a major threat to public and environmental health. Water contamination threatens safe drinking water sources, while air pollution is a known contributor to respiratory disorders and early mortality. Agricultural output and ecosystem health are both at risk due to soil contamination. The accumulation of plastic trash in the world's waterways is a major threat to marine life and ecologies.

Another component of the dilemma is the exhaustion of resources due to excessive use and mining. With a growing human population comes a greater need for the world's limited supply of natural resources. The rate at which we consume the world's resources, from minerals and fossil fuels to forests and fisheries, is exceeding the rate at which they can be replenished. This over use is eroding the sustainability of both renewable and nonrenewable resources. Without major shifts in how we manage our resources, we could deplete Earth's limited resources.

There are significant social and economic aspects to the environmental catastrophe that are often overlooked. Degradation of the natural environment disproportionately affects already disadvantaged populations. Vulnerable communities are disproportionately affected by pollution and natural catastrophes and have less access to resources and protection, making environmental justice an urgent issue. Economic systems that have contributed to environmental degradation must also be rethought. The move towards a more sustainable economy is not only necessary, but also presents a unique chance to spur creativity and new business. Collective and individual efforts are equally important in finding solutions to the global environmental challenge. Countries can work together to tackle climate change because of international accords like the Paris Accord. The government's involvement in creating rules and regulations to limit ecological damage and safeguard natural resources is crucial. However, people and communities can make a big difference by committing to sustainability, working for social and environmental justice, and purchasing from environmentally conscious businesses.

In the midst of this turmoil, technological progress stands as a ray of light. Clean energy alternatives like solar and wind power, as well as sustainable agricultural practises and efficient transportation systems, are just a few examples of how modern technology has the ability to lessen our influence on the environment. Better environmental monitoring and protection is possible with the use of datadriven smart technology.

However, rethinking our relationship with the world is essential to solving the global environmental issue. Sustainability, conservation, and stewardship are urged as new ideals and goals. It's about imagining a world in which humans and other forms of life may coexist peacefully, and where the longterm effects of our actions are taken into account at all times.

This book, "The Fragile Earth: Navigating the Global Environmental Crisis," is written with the intention of equipping its readers with the tools they need to tackle the intricate web of environmental problems we face today. It's a rallying cry for people to wake up and realise the gravity of the situation we're in and get involved. To achieve a future where the delicate Earth is respected, safeguarded, and nurtured, we will investigate the policies, practises, and innovations that can get us there. Within these pages, we will discover accounts of perseverance, suggestions for dealing with urgent problems, and motivation to join a worldwide effort to protect our home planet. Earth is vulnerable, and our future depends on the decisions we make now.

1.2- Historical context and the evolution of environmental awareness.

The Development of Ecology Consciousness and Its Historical Context

Throughout the millennia of human development, people have had a complicated and nuanced interaction with their natural surroundings. There have been many historical, cultural, and technological influences on the development of environmental consciousness, or the recognition that human actions have consequences for the natural environment. This essay explores the origins and development of environmental consciousness, identifying seminal moments, paradigm shifts, and major personalities who have all played a part in shaping our current understanding of environmental challenges.

Ancient Civilizations, a Time of Peaceful Coexistence

Ancient societies lived in greater harmony with their surroundings. Native American and other tribal tribes around the world were highly attentive to their environments. They managed their resources sustainably and adapted their lifestyles to the seasonal cycles of their environments. Native American stewardship values the interconnectedness of all life and the importance of protecting the land for the benefit of future generations.

Even ancient cultures like Greece and Rome were aware of the need of protecting the natural world. Ecological ethics can be traced back to the musings of ancient philosophers like Plato and Aristotle on humanity's place in the natural world. Their thinking was rooted in the tenets of Stoicism and Epicureanism, which advocated for a life in harmony with the natural world and the development of a feeling of environmental responsibility.

Beliefs in Religion and Mythology

Humans' views on the natural world have been shaped by a wide range of religious and mythical notions. Attributing spiritual importance to natural components is common in indigenous belief systems; doing so reinforces a sense of reverence and responsibility. The concept of "dharma" in Hinduism, for example, emphasises conformity with the natural order, while the concept of "stewardship" of the Earth is central to the JudeoChristian tradition. Nature is revered and protected in these and other cultures because it is considered as a manifestation of the divine.

Alteration in Mentality with the Rise of Industrialization

With the dawn of the Industrial Revolution in the 18th and 19th centuries, human communities underwent dramatic transformations. The steam engine and mass industry, two examples of technological progress, fueled extraordinary economic growth, but at a high cost to the environment. Natural areas were replaced by manmade structures like mines and towns as urbanisation and industrialization spread. There was a clear increase in environmental problems including pollution and deforestation and erosion as a result of these developments.

The Romantic Movement appeared during this time period and promoted humankind's reintegration with the natural world. William Wordsworth and Samuel Taylor Coleridge, among others, emphasised the spiritual and emotional importance of pristine landscapes in their works that praised nature's aesthetic value. The conservation movement owes much to this upsurge in environmental awareness and activism.

An Early Attempt at Conservation
Formal conservation efforts emerged in the late 19th and early 20th centuries. Many notable Americans, like President Theodore

Roosevelt and Sierra Club founder John Muir, fought for the protection of America's natural attractions. Their efforts led to the creation of national parks and the preservation of huge areas of natural habitat. As the world's first national park, Yellowstone paved the way for the protection of natural spaces around the globe when it was established in 1872.

In a similar vein, the early 20th century saw the birth of the Audubon Society and the National Parks Conservation Association. Their goals included spreading environmental awareness, advocating for protection of natural areas, and conserving species. Awareness of the scarcity of many resources, the importance of protecting endangered species, and the worth of wildness to future generations all contributed to the conservation movement's momentum.

The Environmental Movement and "Silent Spring"

The release of Rachel Carson's seminal work, "Silent Spring," in 1962 represented a watershed moment in the development of ecological consciousness in the middle of the twentieth century. The contemporary environmental movement may be traced back to Carson's expose on the dangers of pesticide DDT and other chemical contaminants. The public outcry that "Silent Spring" prompted led to the eventual outlawing of DDT and the establishment of the Environmental Protection Agency (EPA) in the United States.

The 1970s were a watershed year for the rise of environmental consciousness and movement. On the first Earth Day, April 22, 1970, millions of people in the United States and throughout the world showed their support for protecting the environment. A slew of environmental laws, such as the Clean Air Act, the Clean Water Act, and the Endangered Species Act, were passed after this disaster. These statutes marked a major change in attitude towards the necessity of systemic solutions to environmental problems.

Worldwide Ecology Movement

As climate change and biodiversity loss became pressing global challenges in the second half of the 20th century, environmental consciousness expanded beyond national lines. To address these issues and promote sustainable development, the United Nations held the inaugural Earth Summit in Stockholm in 1972. The Rio Earth Summit in 1992 and the Paris Agreement in 2015 both owe a great deal to the precedent set by this gathering for international cooperation on environmental challenges.

Sustainability and Climate Change

Climate change, sustainable development, and biodiversity conservation have all received increased attention as pressing issues in the 21st century. The IPCC was formed in 1988 to evaluate the scientific consensus on climate change, and its reports have been essential in shaping international climate policy. People's attention has been focused on climate change mitigation and protection of the world for future generations thanks to the efforts of climate activists and groups like Greta Thunberg and Extinction Rebellion.

The concept of sustainable development has emerged as a central theme in the green movement. To promote economic growth, social fairness, and environmental protection while also tackling global concerns, the United Nations approved the Sustainable Development Goals (SDGs) in 2015. The SDGs emphasise a comprehensive approach to global concerns, recognising the need to strike a balance between economic development, environmental stewardship, and social wellbeing.

Technology's Impact

There has been a double effect of technology on the development of ecological consciousness. One way in which it has contributed to environmental damage is through the energy and resources it has required in manufacturing. However, technological advancements have made it possible to keep an eye on the environment, gather relevant data, and develop novel approaches to sustainability. We are better able to monitor and fix environmental problems because to developments in remote sensing, data analytics, and renewable energy technology.

A Worldwide Uprising

Concern for the environment has spread from localised areas to become a worldwide phenomenon. An increased sense of global community and shared environmental responsibility has resulted from the widespread use of social media and other forms of digital communication. Politics, business, education, and civil society are all more concerned with environmental issues, which has an impact on policy, corporate sustainability programmes, and individual lifestyle choices.

Personal Initiative and Accountability

Recent years have seen a shift towards a greater value placed on personal initiative and accountability. In recent years, there has been a rise in environmental consciousness, prompting many people to reconsider their personal environmental impact and make positive changes towards a greener way of life. Recycling, trash reduction, energy conservation, and environmentally conscious purchasing are now mainstream practises. A more ecofriendly and accountable society is reflected in cultural trends like zero waste, veganism, and minimalism.

Teaching and lobbying
From kindergarten through college, education has played a crucial role in spreading environmental consciousness. Sustainability initiatives and academic research on the environment

Chapter 2.
The Consequences of Climate Change

2.1 Detailed examination of climate change and its consequences.

Analysis of the Causes and Effects of Global Warming

The issue of climate change is one of the most pressing worldwide problems we face today. Ecosystems, weather patterns, economy, and cultures are all impacted by this broad and intricate set of problems. This indepth look at climate change and its effects will delve into the science behind the phenomenon, identify its root causes and contributors, and assess its wideranging effects on the natural world, human health, and the global economy.

Climate Change and the Science Behind It

The rise in average temperatures around the world is a major contributor to the planet's changing climate. The increased greenhouse effect, caused in large part by human activities such as the emission of greenhouse gases, is the primary driver of this warming. Trapping more heat from the sun, chemicals including carbon dioxide (CO_2), methane (CH_4), and nitrous oxide (N_2O) raise global average temperatures over time. This understanding of climate change based on scientific research is wellestablished.

The science behind climate change has been thoroughly evaluated by the Intergovernmental Panel on Climate Change (IPCC), an international group of scientists. From what I can gather from their findings, the average surface temperature of Earth has increased by around 1.2 degrees Celsius (2.2 degrees Fahrenheit) since the late 19th century, and this increase is attributable almost entirely to human activity. Temperature records, ice core samples, and computational models are only few of the sources that lend credence to this hypothesis.

What Caused It and What Played a Role

Although many things contribute to climate change, human activities that release greenhouse gases are a major role. Major contributors to these emissions include the following:

1. Fossil Fuel Combustion Most manmade greenhouse gases come from the burning of fossil fuels for use in power plants, cars, and factories. Coal, oil, and gas are all part of this category. The carbon dioxide (CO_2) released as a result of these activities is a major contributor to climate change.

Deforestation, secondly: Deforestation contributes to rising atmospheric CO_2 levels because forests absorb and store carbon. Removal of trees and other vegetation limits the planet's ability to absorb and store carbon dioxide (CO_2).

Agriculture, third: Methane and nitrous oxide, two of the most potent greenhouse gases, are released into the atmosphere as a result of agricultural activities. Methane is produced by livestock, particularly cattle, during digestion, and nitrous oxide is released when synthetic fertilisers are used in farming.

4. Industrial Processes: The manufacturing of cement and the use of synthetic refrigerants are two examples of industrial processes that contribute to global warming.

5. Land Use Changes: The urban heat island effect, caused by urbanisation and landuse changes, can further worsen local warming.

The Effects of Global Warming

Global warming will have farreaching effects on ecosystems, human health, and economies. Some of the most immediate results are:

One, Heating Up Heatwaves are becoming increasingly often and extreme as global temperatures rise. The elderly and people with preexisting health issues are particularly at risk from the devastating effects of these heat waves.

Second, Rising Sea Levels Due to Ice Melt: Glaciers and polar ice caps are melting due to the increasing warmth of the Earth's atmosphere. Because of this, coastal areas, especially those on lower ground, are at greater risk of flooding and erosion. Rising sea levels pose a significant threat to many island states.

Thirdly, Extreme Weather Increases in hurricanes, typhoons, droughts, and floods have all been linked to climate change. Property loss, injuries, and the disruption of daily life are all possible results of such occurrences.

4. Acidification of the Oceans The world's waters are likewise impacted by rising atmospheric CO_2 levels. Ocean acidification is caused by the formation of carbonic acid when CO_2 is dissolved in seawater. The marine ecosystem, including coral reefs and shellfish, suffers as a result.

5. Dwindling Biodiversity The loss of species due to global warming is a serious problem. Many species are in jeopardy of extinction because of the difficulties they are having adapting to the new, unpredictable environment.

Water and Food Safety, Number Six: Food and water distribution systems are vulnerable to climate change. Droughts and floods, brought on by shifts in the frequency and intensity of precipitation, can reduce crop yields and increase the risk of food insecurity.

Furthermore, in areas that rely on glacier meltwater for their water supply, rising temperatures can have a devastating effect.

7. Impacts on Health: The effects of climate change on human health are both immediate and longterm. Heatwaves increase the prevalence of heatrelated disorders including heat stroke. Diseases can spread farther as vectors such as mosquitoes find new places to call home due to shifts in weather patterns.

8. Disruption to the Economy: The effects of climate change on the economy will be severe. Extreme weather events cause economic disruption through damage to infrastructure, decreased agricultural productivity, and higher healthcare costs. Population shifts caused by climate change might further stress alreadystrapped local infrastructure and services.

Security on a National Scale: Threats to national security may be compounded by climate change. Instability and security hazards can be posed on a global scale as a result of resource shortage, forced migration, and the possibility for conflict over decreasing resources.

Strategies for Adaptation and Mitigation

The two main strategies for dealing with climate change are adaptation and mitigation. When it comes to climate change, adaptation entails making plans for and coping with the effects, whereas mitigation emphasises cutting emissions of greenhouse gases. The following are examples of approaches and remedies for dealing with climate change:

Making the Change to Renewable Energy: A crucial mitigation option is the transition away from fossil fuels and towards renewable energy sources like solar, wind, and hydropower. Cleaner energy sources are receiving funding from governments, businesses, and individuals alike.

2. Energy Savings: Energy consumption and emissions can be decreased by increasing efficiency in buildings, transportation, and industry. This includes the use of methods and tools that reduce energy use.

The Third and Fourth Methods of Forestry: Reforestation and rehabilitating damaged land both contribute to carbon sequestration. These measures also help preserve biodiversity.

(4) Environmentally Responsible Farming Reducing emissions and increasing carbon sequestration are both possible outcomes of adopting sustainable farming practises. Methods like notill farming, agroforestry, and organic farming fall under this category.

Emissions can be reduced financially by the use of carbon pricing mechanisms like carbon taxes or capandtrade systems.

6. Adaptation Strategies for a Changing Climate: The effects of climate change must be planned for. This involves making improvements to water management, preparing for natural disasters, and other infrastructure.

The Seventh Benefit of Global Partnerships: International agreements like the Paris Agreement seek to coordinate efforts to cut emissions and control global warming in response to the worldwide threat posed by climate change.

Conclusion

Global warming poses a complex and immediate threat with farreaching effects. The scientific consensus is that human actions, especially the release of greenhouse gases, are the primary causes of this shift. Communities all throughout the world are already feeling the effects of climate change, from higher average temperatures and higher sea levels to more intense weather and negative health effects. However, sustainable development is possible with the help of mitigation and adaptation techniques. We can mitigate the effects of climate change and strengthen our resilience to it by switching to renewable energy, increasing energy efficiency, safeguarding forests, and adopting other climateresilient practises. In order to ensure a healthier, safer, and more sustainable environment for future generations, global cooperation and individual action are vital in the battle against climate change.

2.2 Case studies on extreme weather events, rising temperatures, and melting ice.

Studies of How Global Warming, Rising Temperatures, and Melting Ice Have Affected Individual Communities

Extreme weather, higher temperatures, and the loss of glaciers are all making it clear that climate change is no longer a theoretical risk. These case studies illustrate the effects of these consequences on our planet, its ecosystems, and human society in the here and now.

Hurricane Katrina is the first case study of extreme weather events.

Hurricane Katrina in 2005 was one of the most catastrophic natural disasters in modern history. This hurricane, with winds of up to 155 miles per hour, made landfall in the United States, devastating the city of New Orleans in particular. Over a million people were forced to leave their homes when a major storm surge and levee failure caused widespread flooding.

Rising sea levels and increased ocean temperatures provided the energy needed for Hurricane Katrina to strengthen, contributing to the storm's severity and the destruction it wreaked. The increased frequency and intensity of such catastrophes is consistent with climate models, while it is crucial to stress that individual hurricanes cannot be directly attributed to climate change. Katrina's aftermath highlighted the need for better disaster preparedness and response and the vulnerability of coastal towns to rising sea levels.

The Second Case: Rising Temperatures and European Heatwaves

There was a public health catastrophe and considerable economic losses as a result of a series of heatwaves that hit Europe in the summer of 2003. Tens of thousands of extra deaths were recorded across the continent as a result of the heatwaves, which were characterised by prolonged periods of high temperatures.

Human activity has increased the frequency and intensity of heatwaves, according to scientific studies. Extreme heat was caused in part by a combination of factors, including a warming planet and altered weather patterns. The significance of both adaptation measures to safeguard vulnerable populations and mitigation efforts to curb global warming was brought home by these occurrences.

Third Case Study: The Greenland Ice Sheet and Its Rapid Decline

As global temperatures rise, a major portion of Greenland's massive ice sheet is melting. This melting ice has farreaching repercussions outside of the Arctic. Rising sea levels, exacerbated by increased meltwater runoff, threaten coastal cities around the world.

One of Greenland's fastestmoving glaciers is the Jakobshavn Glacier. Its retreat over the past two decades has accelerated, adding to sea level rise. Climate systems in faraway places may be affected by changes in ocean circulation brought on by the melting ice.

Furthermore, local ecosystems and indigenous groups dependent on hunting and fishing are feeling the effects of Greenland's ice melting. Social, cultural, and economic factors are also affected by the diminished sea ice and changing migration patterns of marine species.

Example 4: Australian Bushfires as an Example of Extreme Weather

Australia has a history of bushfires, but the current one is unique in both size and intensity. Fires ravaged millions of acres of land, burned thousands of homes, and killed people and animals due to the combination of a severe drought, high temperatures, and high winds.

Extreme heat and persistent drought had clear ties to global warming. As temperatures rose, drought conditions worsened, making dry plants more flammable. Large quantities of carbon dioxide were released as a result of the bushfires, adding to the problem of atmospheric warming.

Devastating effects on Australia's ecosystems, biodiversity, and the emotional wellbeing of affected communities resulted from these fires. They also emphasised the importance of preventative measures to reduce fire hazards and adapt to a warming planet.

Case 5: Antarctica's Melting Ice Shelves

Warming ocean waters are a major contributor to the rapid melting of Antarctic ice shelves. The Larsen C Ice Shelf is a particularly worrying case in point. It was the source of A68, one of the world's largest icebergs, in 2017.

The effects of ice shelf collapse are threefold. First, it adds to the global problem of rising sea levels, which endangers all places with coastlines. Second, it can cause the remaining land ice to become unstable, which might accelerate its melting and hasten the increase of sea levels.

This study demonstrates how the loss of Antarctic ice is not a faraway issue but rather a global one, with possible consequences for people and coasts around the world.

Case Study 6: Rising Temperatures and the Great Barrier Reef

The Great Barrier Reef is one of the world's most wellknown and diversified coral reef ecosystems; it is also a UNESCO World Heritage site. However, rising water temperatures have caused coral bleaching episodes, which have had a devastating effect. Corals lose their brilliant colours and eventually die as a result of coral bleaching, which occurs when corals eject the symbiotic algae that feed them with nourishment.

Bleaching on the Great Barrier Reef is caused by climate changerelated increases in water temperature. Longterm effects on marine life and tourism, a major economic engine in the region, were seen after the 2016 and 2017 bleaching events, which devastated more than twothirds of the reef.

The effects of climate change in the real world are illustrated by these case studies. Ecosystems, communities, and economies are all directly and indirectly impacted by extreme weather events, rising temperatures, and melting glaciers. These difficulties highlight the importance of acting quickly to reduce greenhouse gas emissions through individual and collective measures of mitigation and adaptation. We must all work together to lessen the effects of climate change and create a more sustainable and resilient future for Earth and all her inhabitants.

Chapter 3.
We are losing biodiversity and ecosystems.

3.1 Discussion of the loss of biodiversity and its effects.

Impacts of Biodiversity Loss and How to Stop It

The term "biodiversity" is shorthand for "biological diversity," which describes the wide range of organisms found on our planet. It consists of all forms of life and the ecosystems they are a part of, from the tiniest of bacteria to the largest of mammals. While biodiversity is crucial to the wellbeing of our world, it is under siege from new and unprecedented dangers. In this talk, we'll examine the repercussions of biodiversity loss on ecosystems, human societies, and the global community as a whole.

Current Biodiversity Loss Scenarios

Natural and humancaused forces are contributing equally to the rapid decline of biodiversity. Although extinctions have occurred naturally throughout Earth's history, the current rate is believed to be 1,000 times higher than the natural background rate, and this is mostly attributable to human activity.

The destruction and fragmentation of habitats (1): Habitat degradation is a major factor in the extinction of species, and it is largely brought on by human activities like farming, deforestation, and land development. Natural areas are being replaced by urban areas, agricultural land, and manmade structures as human populations grow. Isolation of populations due to habitat fragmentation reduces genetic diversity and increases species' susceptibility to extinction.

Alterations to the Climate: Climate change is also a major influence in declining biodiversity. Temperature increases and changes in precipitation patterns can have farreaching consequences for ecosystems and the distribution and behaviour of a wide variety of species. Some species just can't adjust or relocate fast enough to keep up with the climate's unpredictable shifts.

Ecosystems are negatively impacted by pollution from human activities such as farming, manufacturing, and city living. Damage to ecosystems and human health can result from pollution's contamination of soil, water, and air. It can cause the extinction of rare species and throw ecosystems out of whack.

Invasive species, number four: Bringing in species that aren't native to an area might cause problems for the local fauna in the form of competition, predation, and extinction. It is possible for invasive species to cause the extinction or drastic reduction of native plant and animal life by outcompeting it.

5. Exploitation and excessive harvesting: Populations of commercially valuable species can be depleted and many others put in danger by unsustainable hunting, fishing, and resource collection. Because of this, food webs and ecosystems may be thrown off by overexploitation.

The Consequences of Declining Biodiversity

The loss of biodiversity has farreaching and severe repercussions for ecosystems, human communities, and the global environment as a whole.

(1) The Health and Stability of Ecosystems:

Ecosystems can't function or remain stable without biodiversity. Ecosystems are intricate webs of species interactions that provide a wide range of ecosystem services. Ecosystems lose resilience and become more susceptible to disturbances and shocks like illness, invasive species, and extreme weather when biodiversity decreases.

Second, the threat of starvation:

There can be no food security without biodiversity. Food comes from a wide variety of plant and animal sources. The loss of plant and animal species due to degradation of natural habitats threatens food security and raises prices.

Thirdly, the Depletion of Health Care Supplies:

Natural remedies abound in the world's diverse biodiversity. Natural ingredients are often the starting point for medications. The extinction of species raises the risk that we will never find some of the diseases for which we have no therapy.

Effects on Pollinators, Number Four:

In agriculture, pollinators like bees and butterflies are essential because they help ensure the survival of countless plant species. Pollinator populations are in decline due to habitat loss, pesticide use, and climate change, all of which threaten agricultural output.

5. Loss of Leisure and Cultural Opportunities

Biodiversity plays a crucial role in a wide range of leisure pursuits. Cultural ties to the land are common among indigenous peoples, and biodiversity benefits industries like tourism and outdoor recreation as well as the arts.

Sixth, Feedback Loops in Climate Change:

Through feedback loops, biodiversity loss can hasten global warming. Carbon sinks like forests are crucial because they remove CO_2 from the air and store it for future use. Forest loss and biodiversity loss both impair forests' ability to store carbon, which in turn increases atmospheric concentrations of heattrapping gases.

The Breakdown of Ecosystem Services, Number Seven

Humans rely on ecosystems for a wide variety of goods and services, such as food production, pollination, soil improvement, and temperature control, among many more. Ecosystems' ability to meet human needs is hampered by biodiversity loss, which endangers these services.

8. Enhanced Susceptibility to Illness

Some diseases may become more common as a result of a decline in biodiversity. For instance, the danger of disease transmission to other animals or to people can increase when some species become extinct.

Conservation and risk reduction measures

Conservation and mitigation efforts work together to counteract biodiversity loss and its consequences.

(1) Conservation Lands: The creation and upkeep of protected areas are crucial to the preservation of biodiversity. These protected zones allow ecosystems and species to flourish without interference from humans.

Reforestation, wetland restoration, and coral reef rehabilitation are all examples of habitat restoration projects that can help mitigate harm and speed up species' recoveries.

Thirdly, Sustainable Resource Management can lessen the negative effects of overexploitation and overharvesting of fisheries and forests, for example.

Fourth, biodiversity monitoring is essential for seeing patterns and gauging the success of conservation initiatives.

5. International Agreements: The Convention on Biological Diversity is a prime example of the importance of international agreements for fostering international collaboration in the conservation of biodiversity. These treaties establish goals and rules for the responsible use and preservation of biodiversity.

Sixth, Efforts to Reduce Global Warming: Many species and ecosystems can be shielded from the ill consequences of a warming planet thanks to efforts to reduce greenhouse gas emissions and ameliorate climate change.

7. Awareness in the Community Raising public support for biodiversity conservation requires public awareness and education. Citizens who are wellinformed and actively participate are more inclined to back initiatives that safeguard ecosystems and animal populations.

Conclusion

The extinction of species is a serious threat to all forms of life on Earth. Ecosystems, economics, civilizations, and the natural world as a whole are all negatively impacted. Future generations and the planet's health depend on our generation realising the importance of biodiversity and working together to preserve it. Protecting biodiversity is essential to the health of our planet and not only a moral obligation.

3.2 Profiles of endangered species and vanishing ecosystems.

Species and ecosystems that are at danger of extinction are highlighted.

The current situation of biodiversity is a major cause for alarm, as many species are on the verge of extinction and essential ecosystems are under severe attack. The profiles of several endangered species and the ecosystems they depend on are explored in this article to emphasise the significance of conservation efforts and the necessity of addressing the causes of their decline.

Panthera pardus orientalis, commonly known as the Amur leopard.

There are just about 80 wild Amur leopards left, making it one of the most critically endangered big cat species. The natural habitat of this leopard subspecies includes the Russian Far East and some regions of China. Large rosettes on a white backdrop give this leopard species its distinctive appearance, setting it apart from others in the genus.

Habitat and Dangers:
The Amur leopard lives in temperate woodlands and feeds mostly on wild boars and deer. Their numbers were cut in half due to loss of habitat, illegal hunting, and forest destruction. Sadly, these stunning cats are under danger because to the illegal wildlife trafficking for their skins and bones.

The last Amur leopards and their habitats are being protected thanks to the efforts of conservation organisations. Humanwildlife conflicts can be mitigated by measures including increased antipoaching initiatives, habitat restoration, and community involvement.

Ceratotherium simum cottoni, or the northern white rhinoceros.

The northern white rhinoceros is a symbol of a species in danger of extinction. This subspecies, which was once widespread across East and Central Africa, is now down to just two females—Najin and Fatu—in captivity. Sudan, the last male, died in 2018.

Habitat and Dangers:
The northern white rhino is most at risk from the destruction of its habitat and illegal hunting for its horn. The illegal trade of rhino horn, which is widely thought to have curative effects, has contributed to the extinction of this species.

Conservation Efforts: In vitro fertilisation and surrogate mothers are part of the plan to rescue the northern white rhino. Poaching can only be stopped if the underlying demand for rhino horn is reduced.

Threetoed orangutan from Sumatra (Pongo abelii).

The Sumatran orangutan is endemic to the island of Sumatra in Indonesia and is one of the two species of orangutans in the world. Fewer than 14,000 of these animals are still out there, making them highly endangered.

The biggest threats to the Sumatran orangutan are the destruction of its habitat for palm oil plantations, illicit logging, and the pet trade. Deforestation is increasingly eradicating their habitat.

EnergySaving Measures
Orangutan habitats are being restored and protected, while rescued and rehabilitated orphans and animals seized from the illegal pet trade are receiving care.

Phocoena sinus (the vaquita)

With only about 10 individuals left in the wild, the vaquita is the most critically endangered marine mammal on the planet. Known as the "panda of the sea" for its distinctive black stripes, this tiny porpoise is endemic to the Gulf of California.

Habitat and Dangers:
When gillnets are used to illegally collect totoaba, another endangered species, vaquitas are often caught as bycatch. Totoaba fish are prized for their bladders in Asian markets.

EnergySaving Measures
In order to conserve the vaquita, conservationists must act quickly. The vaquita's habitat is being patrolled and illicit fishing gear is being removed and replaced with legal alternatives.

Number Five: The Amazon Rainforest

The Amazon Rainforest is home to around 10% of all species on Earth, making it one of the most biologically varied ecosystems on the planet. It includes land from nine separate South American countries and has a total area of nearly 6.7 million square kilometres. In addition to providing shelter for a wide variety of animals and plants, this verdant forest also helps to moderate global temperatures.

Threats:
The Amazon Rainforest is mainly threatened by deforestation for purposes such as agriculture, logging, and infrastructure construction. When forests are destroyed, the world loses a wealth of species and their unique genetic and ecological makeup.

Protected areas, sustainable landuse practises, and monitoring and regulating illicit logging and land clearing are all part of the ongoing effort to preserve the Amazon Rainforest.

Sixth, the Great Barrier Reef.

The Great Barrier Reef is the largest coral reef in the world, and it can be found just off the coast of Queensland, Australia. Because of its rich marine life and beautiful coral formations, it has been named a UNESCO World Heritage Site and is considered a priceless treasure around the world.

Threats:
Overfishing, coastal expansion, pollution runoff, and rising sea temperatures are just a few of the many dangers to the Great Barrier Reef's coral. Because it disrupts the entire reef ecosystem, coral bleaching is of particular concern.

Establishing marine protected areas, taking steps to decrease pollution, and conducting continuing scientific research are all examples of conservation efforts aimed at safeguarding the Great Barrier Reef.

Tundra of the Arctic Seventh

Climate change is having a profound effect on the Arctic tundra, a region known for its extreme cold, permafrost, and rare flora and animals. Northern regions of North America, Europe, and Asia are home to this huge and inaccessible ecology.

Threats:
As the Arctic warms, permafrost begins to thaw, producing ecological shifts and the release of previously frozen greenhouse gases. This has an effect on the rare biodiversity of the tundra and adds to global warming.

EnergySaving Measures
Protecting the Arctic's animals and landscapes from the effects of climate change is an important part of conservation efforts.

Supporting international pacts to cut GHG emissions is also part of the job.

Conclusion

The stories of these animals and their disappearing habitats drive home the critical nature of solving the world's biodiversity issue. In addition to diminishing the planet's beauty and diversity, the extinction of species and the collapse of entire ecosystems threatens the delicate balance of life on Earth.

Protecting and conserving threatened ecosystems and animal populations is crucial. To address the core reasons of their decline, we need a combination of conservation efforts, sustainable landuse practises, and international cooperation. To guarantee the continued existence of these extraordinary species and habitats, public education and support for biodiversity conservation are essential. It is our moral obligation to safeguard the diversity of life on Earth for the sake of future generations.

Chapter 4.
Environmental Hazards and Human Health

4.1 Exploration of various forms of pollution (air, water, soil) and their health implications.

Examining the Effects of Environmental Pollution on Human Health

Air pollution, water pollution, and soil pollution are all indicators of pollution, which is a widespread and intricate environmental concern. Air, water, and soil contamination are all sources of pollution that will be examined, along with the devastating effects they have on human health. In order to effectively address the worldwide environmental and public health concerns posed by different types of pollution, it is crucial to comprehend where they come from and what effects they have.

Pollution of the Air

Pollutants in the Air:
Air pollution occurs when harmful pollutants enter the air and have an adverse effect on living things and the environment. It's caused by a wide range of factors, both natural and anthropogenic, including:

First, using up fossil fuels for energy. Industrial activities, transportation, and electricity generation all contribute to air pollution by burning fossil fuels including coal, oil, and natural gas. Carbon dioxide (CO_2), sulphur dioxide (SO_2), nitrogen oxides (NOx), and particulate matter are only some of the air pollutants that are produced as a result of this process.

Second, Agricultural Practises add to air pollution by the release of ammonia and methane from the use of fertilisers, pesticides, and the improper disposal of animal waste.

Thirdly, Industrial Emissions: a variety of air pollutants, such as volatile organic compounds (VOCs), heavy metals, and hazardous chemicals, are released during industrial activities, especially those involving the chemical, manufacturing, and mining industries.

Four, Transportation: Greenhouse gases and other pollutants including nitrogen dioxide (NO2) and fine particulate matter (PM2.5) are emitted from vehicles such as cars, trucks, and planes, making them a major cause of air pollution.

5. Natural Materials: Air pollution can also be caused by natural phenomena like forest fires, volcanic eruptions, and dust storms.

Air pollution's effects on human health:
Many health problems can be attributed to air pollution.

Issues with Breathing: Asthma, bronchitis, and chronic obstructive pulmonary disease (COPD) are only few of the respiratory illnesses that may develop from prolonged exposure to air pollution. The presence of fine particulate matter (PM2.5) might exacerbate these symptoms by penetrating deep into the lungs.

Second, Cardiovascular Disorders: Heart disorders like heart attacks, strokes, and hypertension have been linked to air pollution. Airborne particles and gaseous pollutants can be absorbed into the circulatory system, where they can trigger inflammatory responses and oxidative stress.

Thirdly, Cancer: Polycyclic aromatic hydrocarbons (PAHs), benzene, and formaldehyde are just a few of the air pollutants that have been linked to an increased risk of getting cancer after prolonged exposure.

Children who are exposed to high levels of air pollution may have their lungs develop improperly, which can cause chronic breathing problems later in life.

5. Premature Death: Premature Death has been connected to air pollution in studies. It causes millions of fatalities annually in some areas.

Pollution of Water

Causes of water contamination:
Water pollution occurs when pollutants that are detrimental to living beings enter water sources such rivers, lakes, oceans, and groundwater. Examples of major contributors to water pollution are:

Industrial Discharges: The discharge of pollutants, such as heavy metals, chemicals, and poisons, from industrial activity can contaminate water bodies.

Second, Agricultural Runoff contributes to water pollution by carrying pollutants such as pesticides, fertilisers, and animal faeces from farmlands.

Thirdly, Municipal Wastewater: Contaminants in sewage and municipal effluents can make their way into drinking water if they aren't properly handled.

Fourth, Oil Spills pose serious dangers to marine ecosystems and human health through the accidental or intentional release of oil and other harmful chemicals into water bodies.
5 Toxic chemicals used in mining operations can seep into groundwater and aquatic ecosystems.

Leachate from landfills, which may include hazardous materials, can seep into groundwater and surface water. 6.
Effects of Polluted Water on Human Health:
Negative effects on human health due to water pollution include:
1. Diseases Transmitted by Water: Diseases like cholera, dysentery, and hepatitis can be spread through ingesting contaminated water that is home to bacteria, viruses, and parasites.

Second, Chemical Exposure: People who drink dirty water can develop a wide range of health issues, including brain impairment, organ failure, and cancer, due to their exposure to the chemicals and heavy metals found in the water.

3. Respiratory Problems: Toxins produced by harmful algal blooms, which flourish in dirty water, can become airborne and have an adverse effect on people's respiratory health.

4. Developmental and Reproductive Disorders Some contaminants in drinking water have been linked to birth defects and other health problems in children.

Indirectly affecting human health and livelihoods, water pollution can devastate aquatic ecosystems and cause fisheries to collapse and water quality to deteriorate.

Pollution of the Soil
Causes of soil contamination:
When pollutants that are bad for people and the environment find their way into the soil, this is called soil pollution. Some typical causes of soil contamination are:

Industrial Operations 1.

4.2 The role of industry, agriculture, and transportation in pollution.

Factors Contributing to Air Pollution from Manufacturing, Farming, and Driving

The effects of pollution on human health, ecosystems, and the world as a whole are widespread and serious. The three most significant contributors to pollution are the industrial sector, the agricultural sector, and the transportation sector. In this talk, we'll examine the ways in which these industries contribute to air, water, and soil pollution, as well as the steps we may take to lessen these consequences.

Air Pollution and Industrial Activity:

Pollution Origins:
The air pollution is mostly caused by the industrial operations. Industrial facilities such as power plants, factories, and chemical processing plants generate many different types of air pollutants.

First, there's Particulate Matter (PM), which includes both fine and coarse particles and can be breathed into the respiratory system, causing all sorts of problems.

Acid rain and respiratory issues are caused by sulphur dioxide (SO_2), which is released when fossil fuels are burned.

Third, Nitrogen Oxides (NOx), which are produced during combustion and add to smog, ozone depletion, and respiratory problems.

Ozone and smog at ground level are formed when volatile organic compounds (VOCs) emitted by factories combine with other contaminants.

Heavy Metals: Heavy metals, such as mercury, lead, and cadmium, are released into the air during industrial processes and can be harmful to human health.

Repercussions on Health:
The health effects of pollution from industrial sources include:

1. Respiratory Problems: Particulate matter and volatile organic compounds (VOCs) are two types of air pollutants that can aggravate respiratory conditions including asthma and bronchitis.

Cardiovascular Disorders: Cardiovascular disorders, such as heart attacks and strokes, are linked to exposure to air pollution.

Thirdly, Cancer Risk: Prolonged exposure to certain industrial toxins, such as benzene and formaldehyde, raises the probability of developing the disease.

4. Neurological Effects: Some industrial pollutants, such as lead and mercury, can have an effect on the neurological system, causing problems with learning and development in young children.

5. Environmental Impact: Smog, acid rain, and climate change are all caused in part by industrial emissions, which also have an effect on ecosystems and biodiversity.

Prevention Measures
The following pollution control measures are essential for lowering industrial air pollution:

One Example of a Cleaner Technology Emissions from manufacturing can be drastically cut back if cleaner, more energyefficient technology were to be implemented.

It is the responsibility of governments to impose strict air quality standards and regulations, including enforcing emission caps for factories.

Thirdly, Pollution Control Equipment, such as scrubbers and catalytic converters, can be installed to capture and reduce pollutants.

Greenhouse gas emissions and the environmental effect of industrial processes can be lowered by switching from fossil fuels to renewable energy sources.

5. Public Awareness: Educating the public on the negative impacts of industrial pollution on human health and the environment can help garner more wellinformed support for clean energy and emissions reduction initiatives.

The Impact of Farming on Water Quality:

Pollution Origins:
Agricultural runoff, which includes but is not limited to the following, is a major source of agriculturallyrelated water pollution:

Herbicides and pesticides, first. The contamination of both surface and groundwater is a potential outcome of using these herbicides on crops.

Fertilisers, number two. Nutrient contamination occurs when water supplies become contaminated with excessive amounts of nutrients from fertilisers, especially nitrogen and phosphorus.

Thirdly, Animal manure: Untreated or poorly managed animal manure from livestock farms can introduce harmful bacteria and organic matter into water supplies.

Repercussions on Health:

Agricultural water pollution can cause a wide range of medical issues.

1. Diseases Transmitted by Water: Diseases including dysentery, cholera, and diarrhoea are all caused by pathogens and germs in contaminated water.

(2) Dangerous Algal Blooms Harmful algal blooms, caused by an excess of nutrients in water bodies, can be detrimental to human health and aquatic ecosystems due to the toxins they produce.

Thirdly, Endocrine Disruption can occur when chemical contaminants in agriculture mess with human hormones and development.

4. Risk of Cancer: Agriculture pesticides and herbicides may contain carcinogenic chemicals and leak into groundwater supplies.

Prevention Measures
Agricultural water contamination can be reduced by the following measures:

Recommended Actions (RAs): 1. BMPs: Agricultural pollution can be decreased by advocating for the use of best management practises (BMPs), such as reduced pesticide use, controlled fertiliser application, and effective waste management.

Second, "Buffer Zones": In order to prevent agricultural runoff from reaching vulnerable aquatic areas, buffer zones should be established along water bodies.

Promoting sustainable farming practises like organic agriculture and notill farming, for example, can lessen the need for chemical fertilisers and pesticides and cut down on soil erosion.

4. Restrictions and Supervision In order to protect water quality and the ecosystem, the government must strictly regulate and monitor agricultural practises.

5. Education and Outreach: It is crucial to increase farmers' and the general public's understanding of the relevance of good agricultural practises in reducing water pollution.

Pollution from vehicles and the ground:

Transportation, especially that which runs on fossil fuels, is a major contributor to soil pollution due to:

1. Emissions and Spills: Pollutants such heavy metals, oil, and petrol released by vehicle emissions can pollute the land.

Secondly, Road Salts Deicing salts used on roadways during the winter can accumulate in the soil, decreasing its fertility and quality if used year after year.

Thirdly, Airborne Particles Related to Traffic When these particles fall to the ground, they may bring with them contaminants that are bad for the soil.

Repercussions on Health:
Human health, agricultural productivity, and ecological sustainability are all affected by soil contamination caused by vehicles.

Polluted soil can contaminate crops and food products, putting people at risk of exposure to toxic chemicals. 1.

Second, Declining Soil Fertility Agricultural outputs may be negatively impacted by contaminants that reduce soil fertility and productivity.

3. Impact on Ecosystems Pollution of the soil can have negative effects on the biodiversity and ecosystem services provided by terrestrial ecosystems and the creatures that call the soil home.

Prevention Measures
The following measures are crucial for lowering transportationrelated soil pollution:

Reduce emissions and soil contamination by switching to cleaner transportation options like electric vehicles or those that run on alternative fuels.

Procedures for Road Repairs: Limiting the use of deicing salts and promptly cleaning up spills and leaks are two key components of good road maintenance that can help prevent soil contamination.

3. Environmental Impact Assessment: It is critical for infrastructure planning to evaluate the possible soil pollution concerns posed by transport projects and to take steps to minimise them.

Avoiding the construction of roads and other infrastructure in environmentally sensitive areas is one example of how land use planning can lessen the toll that traffic has on soil quality.

To reduce the negative effects of mobility on the environment, it is important to raise public awareness about the importance of regular vehicle maintenance.

Conclusion:

Pollution has many causes, but three major contributors are industrial processes, agricultural practises, and transportation modes. Accepting the

Chapter 5.
Scarcity of resources as a result of excessive use

5.1 Examination of the overexploitation of natural resources.

The Effects of Excessive Use of Natural Resources

Our planet's ecosystems, biodiversity, and the health of human societies are all threatened by the over use of its natural resources, making this a pressing environmental concern. This analysis will go into the meaning of overexploitation, its many forms, and the severe effects it has on ecosystems and social systems. More sustainable resource management and solutions to this urgent problem will also be investigated.

Acquiring an Awareness of Exploitation

When natural resources are used, extracted, or consumed at rates faster than they can be replenished by the planet, this is known as overexploitation. It is possible for this to apply to renewable and nonrenewable resources alike, such as fisheries, forests, minerals, water, and even fossil fuels. Excessive demand and consumption are typically the result of economic, technological, and societal issues that contribute to overexploitation.

Signs of Excessive Exploitation:

First, the problem of overfishing. The overfishing of the world's oceans is a prime illustration of the negative effects of this practise. Many coastal communities have had their food security and livelihoods threatened by the decline of fish populations brought on by unsustainable fishing practises such illegal fishing, bycatch, and the deployment of harmful gear.

Second, deforestation occurs when forests are cut down at an unsustainable rate and the land is used for things like agriculture, urban sprawl, and timber. Deforestation is increasing at an alarming rate, threatening forest ecosystems that are vital for carbon sequestration and biodiversity support.

3. Limited Water Supply: Falling water tables and greater competition for scarce freshwater resources are the results of overextraction of groundwater, which is typically the result of unsustainable irrigation practises and industrial use.

The extraction of minerals and valuable metals like rare earth elements and gold often leads to the destruction of habitat, pollution, and the depletion of nonrenewable resources, which brings us to our next point.

Fifthly, Fossil Fuels: Depleting scarce resources and adding to climate change are two negative outcomes of using fossil fuels like coal, oil, and natural gas for energy generation and transportation.

The Consequences of Abuse:

Overexploitation has indirect and direct repercussions for ecosystems, communities, and the global economy.

Effects on the Environment:

Loss of Biodiversity: 1. Species that are hunted, fished, or harvested for their resources are particularly vulnerable to the effects of overexploitation, which can lead to their decline and eventual extinction. Ecosystems and food webs are negatively impacted by this decline in biodiversity.

2. Damage to Habitat Forests are cut down, wetlands are drained, and fish stocks in the oceans are depleted as a result of human activity. This has consequences for biodiversity as well as the environmental services provided by these areas.

Thirdly, Climate Change: Changes in temperature, precipitation patterns, and sea level are all effects of global warming and climate change, which are exacerbated by the release of greenhouse gases from the combustion of fossil fuels.

Fourthly, "Pollution" Heavy metals released during mining operations and wastewater discharged during fishing and agriculture are two examples of how overexploitation of resources can lead to pollution.

Economic and Social Consequences

One, Food Safety: Communities along the coast that rely heavily on seafood may go hungry if fish stocks are depleted due to overfishing or poor management.

Communities whose economies are tied to resourcebased businesses like forestry or agriculture may struggle if those resources are depleted.

Thirdly, Conflict and Migration arise when people are unable to meet their basic needs because of a lack of resources such as food, water, and shelter.

4. Economic Costs: Overexploitation leads to economic costs such as the requirement for environmental remediation, the loss of ecosystem services, and the possibility of resource scarcity that impacts industries and supply chains.

Solutions to the problem of overexploitation:

It will take a combination of legislation, technology, and sociological shifts to solve the problem of overexploitation.

1. Environmentally Responsible Resource Management It is crucial to adopt sustainable practises for managing resources. Overfishing can be reduced through measures such as limiting catch sizes, encouraging reforestation and sustainable farming practises, and strictly enforcing existing laws.

Innovations in Technology 2: Technology may play a crucial role in resource management. Using sustainable fishing gear, cuttingedge monitoring and data analysis, and precision agriculture techniques, we can lessen the environmental impact of resource extraction.

Thirdly, Safe Zones: Protected areas, marine reserves, and conservation zones help ecosystems recover from overexploitation by safeguarding vital habitats.

4. Teaching the General Public More people may back conservation initiatives if they are made more aware of the negative effects of overexploitation and the value of sustainable practises.

Fifthly, Enforcement and Regulation: Overexploitation of natural resources can be avoided if governments pass and strictly enforce appropriate rules. Strong deterrents can be created by applying penalties for illicit resource exploitation and fishing.

Cooperative efforts on a global scale The successful management and protection of many resources requires cooperation across national boundaries. Collaboration on resource conservation is made easier through treaties and agreements.

Gathering Information and Conducting Studies If you want to know where your resources stand, how they're evolving, and how to best manage them, you need to conduct consistent research and keep meticulous records.

Stories of Achievement

Some major victories have resulted from efforts to curb exploitative practises:

Several whale species have made a comeback from the verge of extinction thanks to international bans on whaling.

Second, the creation of marine parks like the Great Barrier Reef Marine Park has helped to preserve marine ecosystems around the world.

Sustainable Agriculture, which includes organic farming and agroforestry, has played a role in curbing deforestation and preserving soil quality.

Overfishing has been reduced thanks to better management of fish stocks and the use of technology like GPS tracking.

Conclusion:

The overexploitation of natural resources is a pressing problem with farreaching effects on ecology, culture, and the economy as a whole. It will need a concerted effort from governments, businesses, communities, and individuals to overcome this obstacle. We can achieve a more equitable and longlasting relationship with Earth's resources if we adopt sustainable resource management practises, embrace technology and innovation, and raise public knowledge and support for conservation.

5.2 Sustainable alternatives and the importance of resource conservation.

Sustainable Options and the Value of Limiting Consumption of Resources

The notion of sustainability has risen to popularity as the world attempts to address the effects of resource depletion and environmental deterioration. Sustainability is more than just a catchphrase; it provides a necessary framework for dealing with the difficulties caused by excessive consumption and the misuse of natural resources. In this investigation, we'll learn why it's so important to preserve our natural resources, what it is to be sustainable, and what options we have for taking a more ecofriendly approach to the future.

Why It's So Crucial to Reduce Waste:

When natural resources are used in a sustainable and responsible manner, they can be preserved for future generations. It's crucial to environmental preservation and longterm economic growth. Several views are necessary to fully appreciate the significance of resource conservation:

1. Saving Species from Extinction The health of ecosystems is crucial to the production of many commodities. The biodiversity and abundance of species that rely on these environments are safeguarded thanks to conservation efforts.

Protecting Ecosystem Services Clean air and water, agricultural pollination, and climate management are just a few of the many vital services provided by healthy ecosystems to humankind. The availability of these services is guaranteed by the practise of resource conservation.

Climate Change Mitigation (3) Carbon dioxide is absorbed and stored by many types of natural resources, including forests and wetlands. By protecting these crucial ecosystems, resource conservation helps slow global warming.

4. Preventing Resource Depletion: By conserving resources, we avoid their depletion, which can cause scarcity, price instability, and conflicts over access to limited resources.

By reducing the social and economic consequences of resource depletion and pollution, sustainable resource usage benefits local economies and people's ability to make a living.

LongTerm Happiness(6) Taking measures to preserve our natural resources is like saving for the future. By keeping supplies in check, we can ensure that future generations inherit a planet in better health.

Sustainability, as a Concept:

In order to ensure that future generations will be able to meet their own requirements, sustainability takes into account not just economic but also social and environmental considerations. The term "sustainability" refers to three interrelated aspects:

The First Principle of Economic Permanence Responsible consumerism, investment in clean technologies, and ethical corporate practises are all encouraged in this dimension with the goal of sustaining and improving economic wellbeing.

The Social Sustainability Individual and community happiness and contentment are at the heart of social sustainability's focus. It aims to build societies where everyone has access to things like healthcare, education, and housing.

Sustainability in the Environment, Third: Responsible use of natural resources, preservation of ecosystems, and mitigation of environmental degradation are at the heart of environmental sustainability. The overarching goal is to ensure that Earth can continue to sustain life and human endeavours.

The "triple bottom line," which encompasses all three of these factors, is a popular metaphor for the holistic strategy that must be employed to achieve sustainability.

Ecological Substitutes

The environmental impact, resource depletion, and progress towards a more sustainable future can all be mitigated by the use of various sustainable alternatives and practises. Some instances are as follows:

1. Renewable Energy Sources: Switching from fossil fuels to renewables like solar, wind, and hydropower lowers carbon dioxide emissions, slows the progression of global warming, and preserves limited supplies of energy sources like coal and oil.

To minimise resource consumption and energy costs while minimising environmental impacts, it is important to increase energy efficiency in buildings, transportation, and industrial activities.

Organic farming, crop rotation, and agroforestry are all examples of sustainable agriculture practises that help preserve soil quality, conserve water, and lessen the need of artificial fertilisers and pesticides.

Circular Economy, Number Four By reusing, recycling, and repurposing materials and goods, the concept of a circular economy helps to reduce waste and preserve natural resources.

5. Green Building Design: Sustainable architecture and building design make use of renewable energy sources, ecofriendly materials, and other means to lessen their negative effects on the environment.

Ecofriendly transportation options include electric vehicles, public transportation, and nonmotorized options like biking and walking.

7. Water Conservation: Preserving water supplies and safeguarding aquatic ecosystems can be accomplished by the widespread use of watersaving technology and practises in agricultural, industrial, and residential settings.

The availability of wood and forest resources can be guaranteed for the foreseeable future by engaging in sustainable forestry practises such selective logging and reforestation.

Reducing, reusing, and recycling materials can help cut down on waste and raw material consumption, which brings us to point number nine, Waste Reduction.

Sustainability Obstacles & Challenges:

Despite the undeniable advantages of sustainability and resource conservation, a number of obstacles must be overcome in order to hasten the shift to a more sustainable global society:

ShortTerm Goals (1): Investments and efforts in resource conservation are hampered by the fact that many individuals, businesses, and governments put shortterm gains ahead of longterm sustainability.

Culture of the Consumer 2 Resource depletion and environmental deterioration may result from a consumer culture that encourages wasteful spending and quick product discard.

Lacks in Policy and Regulation 3. Sustainable practises and resource conservation can be hampered by inadequate policies, insufficient laws, and an absence of enforcement.

The external environmental costs of resource depletion and pollution are often not taken into account by economic systems, which tend to favour resourceintensive companies.

5. Insufficient Knowledge and Training It is difficult to motivate people to make changes on the personal and societal levels since so few people understand the significance of sustainability and resource conservation.

Addressing global concerns like climate change and biodiversity loss calls for worldwide collaboration and agreements, which can be difficult to achieve. 6. Global Coordination.

Conclusion:

To solve the urgent environmental problems we confront today, resource conservation and longterm sustainability are cornerstone concepts. A more egalitarian, environmentally responsible, and affluent future for current and future generations can be achieved through the adoption of sustainable alternatives and practises, the promotion of responsible consumption and production, and the overcoming of barriers to sustainability.

Chapter 6.
Aspects of Society and the Economy

6.1 Analysis of how environmental issues intersect with social and economic factors.

A Look at the Intersection of Environmental, Social, and Economic Factors

There is a complex web of interdependencies between environmental concerns and other social and economic elements that shapes the world in which we live. The "socioeconomic nexus," the point at which social and economic issues meet, is the focus of this investigation into environmental problems. With this information in hand, we can better address environmental concerns while also advancing social justice and economic growth.

One, the effects of climate change on society and the economy.

To illustrate how environmental concerns intersect with social and economic problems, consider climate change, which is primarily fueled by emissions of greenhouse gases. Its repercussions reach far and wide in social and economic circles:

Catastrophic Weather: Increases in the frequency and severity of natural disasters like hurricanes, droughts, and floods can cause widespread disruption, infrastructure damage, and financial losses.

Safety from Starvation: As a result of climate change, disadvantaged groups may face higher food prices, shortages of staple foods, and threats to their ability to eat healthy and safely.

Implications for Health: Temperature shifts and the proliferation of vectorborne diseases (such as malaria and dengue) pose health threats, impacting healthcare infrastructure and possibly raising mortality rates.

Disparities in Economic Status: The effects of climate change tend to be felt most acutely by vulnerable and marginalised people, thus widening already existing socioeconomic gaps.

Conflict and emigration: Migration due to climaterelated upheaval can exacerbate resource scarcity, power imbalances, and societal unrest.

2. Economic Development and the Effects of Limited Resources:

Water, minerals, and arable land are only few of the natural resources whose depletion can have a negative effect on economic growth and social stability.

Scarcity of water threatens food production, manufacturing, and human survival. Constraints on economic development, disruptions to livelihoods, and social instability are all linked to water scarcity.

Mineral Resource Deficiency The rising expense of extracting nonrenewable minerals has consequences for manufacturing, building infrastructure, and creating energy.

Erosion of Soil Degradation of arable land can have a negative impact on food production and rural incomes.

Economic and energy security depend on the accessibility and affordability of energy sources like fossil fuels and renewable energy.

Third, the repercussions of biodiversity loss on society and the economy:

There are serious social and economic consequences to the continuing decline of biodiversity.

Services provided by ecosystems The ability of ecosystems to perform vital functions like pollination, water purification, and carbon sequestration can be compromised by a decline in biodiversity.

Sectors of the Economy: Agriculture, fishing, and the pharmaceutical industry are just a few of the many economic spheres that benefit from biodiversity. Damage to these sectors and supply chain disruptions may result from its loss.

Native American and Ethnic Groups: Indigenous and local communities are disproportionately impacted by biodiversity loss, which threatens their culture, traditional knowledge, and means of subsistence.

Travel & Tourism The tourism sector benefits greatly from places with abundant biodiversity and thriving ecosystems. Local businesses and tourism are vulnerable to the loss of biodiversity.

Fourth, environmental fairness and social equity:

Social justice and equity are intertwined with environmental concerns since vulnerable populations are disproportionately affected by environmental hazards.

Toxic Exposure: Lowincome communities and communities of colour have a greater likelihood of exposure to toxic substances because they are more likely to reside in close proximity to hazardous waste sites, industrial facilities, and polluted areas.

Conditions of the Air: Lowincome communities are disproportionately impacted by the poor air quality in metropolitan areas, which is caused by factors such as industrial pollutants and transportation.

Disparities in access to green areas and environment have been linked to health inequalities because of their positive effects on both physical and mental health.

When it comes to climate change's effects, such as high heat events and sea level rise, vulnerable populations like the elderly and lowincome communities are particularly at risk.

5. The Transition to Renewable Energy and Its Economic Benefits:

Opportunities for economic development and employment creation exist in the shift to renewable energy sources like solar and wind power.

The Green Economy: Employment prospects in the renewable energy sector contribute to economic growth and help lower unemployment rates.

Independent Power Sources Energy economics are affected by the shift to renewable energy sources because of the increased security and decreased reliance on foreign oil and fossil fuels.

Technology and Innovation: Clean energy and environmentally friendly technology development can help propel economic growth and development.

Adaptation and Mitigation: Renewable energy investment is critical for reducing the impacts of climate change and preparing communities to deal with its aftermath.

6. Environmental protection and environmentally sound farming:

Environmental problems can be solved while also bolstering economic and social prosperity through the use of conservation and sustainable agriculture practises.

Services provided by ecosystems Ecosystem services, such as those provided by purified water, fertile soil, and pest management, are at risk if natural ecosystems are not protected.

Sustainable Agriculture: Both the environment and agricultural economies gain when farmers adopt sustainable farming practises include reducing soil erosion, chemical runoff, and the use of synthetic pesticides and fertilisers.

Food Networks in Your Area Food security can be improved, rural development aided, and greenhouse gas emissions from longdistance transportation cut down by investing in local food systems and smallscale agriculture.

Seventh, Waste Management and the Circular Economy:

Moving towards a circular economy, in which resources and materials are reused, recycled, and repurposed, can have positive effects on people's lives and the economy.

Waste minimization The environmental and financial costs of garbage disposal can be reduced with efficient trash management and recycling.

Effective Use of Available Materials Resource efficiency is promoted in a circular economy, which helps cut down on use of both primary resources and energy.

The recycling and reprocessing sectors foster employment creation and contribute to an expanding circular economy.

New ideas: Innovation in product design, waste minimization, and ecofriendly enterprise strategies are all encouraged by the concepts of the circular economy.

8. Market Pressures and Environmental Regulations:

The interaction of environmental concerns with social and economic aspects is heavily influenced by government policies and market forces.

Legal Procedures Industries and businesses may be affected by environmental restrictions that affect their operations, emissions, and resource use.

Government subsidies and incentives for alternative energy, environmentally friendly farming, and conservation practises can have a significant impact on market behaviour and economic outcomes.

Business models and organisational structures must adapt to meet the growing demand for environmentally friendly goods and services.

6.2 The impact on marginalized communities and potential solutions.

Consequences for Socially Weakened Groups and Possible Responses

The social and economic repercussions of environmental problems do not fall equally on all members of society. Environmental impacts are often borne disproportionately by marginalised communities, who are characterised by lower income levels, limited access to resources, and diminished political power. In this analysis, we'll look at the special problems that disadvantaged groups have, and at some of the ways those problems can be fixed.

The Environmental Disparities Impacting Vulnerable Populations:

Communities at the bottom of the socioeconomic ladder, communities of colour, indigenous communities, and those in economically depressed areas are disproportionately affected by environmental injustices. A number of interrelated social, economic, and political variables contribute to these inequalities. These communities suffer a number of serious problems, including:

Exposure to Toxins Statistically, lowincome neighbourhoods are located closer to polluting businesses and factories. Because of their close closeness to the source, they face greater hazards to their health and the environment from toxic substances and contaminants.

Condition of the Air: Many underprivileged groups are concentrated in polluted metropolitan cores. Problems with breathing and heart health are exacerbated by industrial emissions, traffic pollution, and a lack of green space.

Thirdly, Limited Access to Green Spaces: Residents of lowincome communities have less access to parks, green spaces, and natural places, limiting their options for leisure time activities, physical fitness, and emotional health.

The elderly and lowincome groups are particularly susceptible to the effects of climate change, such as high heat events and sea level rise, because they lack the financial and physical resources to prepare for these changes.

5. Food Deserts: Food deserts form when people in lowincome areas don't have easy access to affordable, nutritious food. This can lead to poor eating habits and health issues.

Sixthly, Lack of Water and Its Quality: Inadequate access to clean water and sanitation services is a major contributor to the prevalence of waterborne illnesses and other health problems in marginalised groups.

7. Displacement and Gentrification: Environmental changes, such as rising sea levels or urban development, can displace marginalised people and contribute to gentrification, which in turn forces longtime inhabitants out of their neighbourhoods.

Possible Methods to Improve the Environment:

Achieving environmental and social fairness requires addressing environmental injustices and reducing the disproportionate burdens experienced by marginalised communities. There are a number of approaches that might be taken to address these problems:

First, we must enact and execute environmental justice rules that are designed to safeguard atrisk populations and distribute environmental advantages and disadvantages fairly.
    Perform environmental impact assessments to determine how marginalised groups may be impacted by proposed policies, initiatives, or laws.

Foster community participation in decisionmaking processes relating to environmental challenges, giving locals a voice in how their neighbourhoods are governed.

Help local groups and initiatives that promote environmental fairness and solve environmental problems in their communities.

Transition to clean and renewable energy sources like wind and solar power to minimise emissions and pollution in underserved populations. 3. Clean Energy and Pollution Reduction.

More stringent emission restrictions and pollution mitigation measures should be implemented in the vicinity of atrisk communities.

Invest in green infrastructure like urban parks and greenways to increase people's proximity to nature, better the quality of the air we breathe, and provide us more places to get some exercise.

Encourage longterm city planning that gives lowincome communities top priority for lowcost housing, public transportation, and shared amenities.

5. Education and Awareness: Offer programmes that raise people's consciousness of environmental problems and health dangers, enabling them to make wellinformed decisions about their own living situations.

Incorporate environmental studies into classroom instruction to raise future generations' awareness and capacity for responsible action.

To ensure that longterm inhabitants may remain in their neighbourhoods during development and regeneration, it is important to create affordable housing schemes and antigentrification measures.

Protect lowincome neighbourhoods from eviction by instituting antigentrification policies like rent control and community land trusts.

7. Clean Water and Sanitation Increase the availability of potable water, proper toilets, and sewage disposal systems in underserved areas.

Stricter restrictions and more thorough testing are needed to address water contamination issues.

8. Food Access Initiatives Back efforts to get fresh, healthy, and cheap food to marginalised regions, eliminating "food deserts" and encouraging healthier diets.

9. Climate Resilience and Adaptation Spend money on infrastructure improvements, early warning systems, and disaster preparation programmes to help vulnerable populations adapt to the effects of climate change.

As the clean energy and environmental sectors continue to expand, it is important to ensure that inhabitants of underserved communities have access to employment training and workforce development programmes in these fields.

Eleventh, Healthcare Access: Reduce health inequalities caused by environmental exposures and increase access to healthcare services in underprivileged communities.

Data Collection and Transparency Collect and share information on environmental inequalities and health outcomes for underserved populations in order to facilitate the use of empirical evidence in policy and resource decisions.

The Flint Water Crisis as a Case Study in Environmental Justice

As a tragic illustration of environmental injustice, the situation in Flint is a prime example. Lead and other toxins entered the water system after the city of Flint, Michigan, shifted to using the Flint River as its primary water source in 2014. Most of Flint's population is African American, and many of them are struggling to make ends meet.

The crisis brought into focus the ways in which social, economic, and ecological variables all interact with one another. Children's elevated blood lead levels highlighted the lack of access to safe water and the failure to address citizen concerns about water quality. This incident highlighted the critical importance of enacting environmental justice measures, fostering selfdetermination within communities, and investing in reliable water supply systems.

Conclusion:

In order to establish a more equitable and sustainable future, we must work together to correct the environmental inequalities that disproportionately affect vulnerable populations. Environmental justice legislation, community involvement, sustainable energy efforts, green infrastructure, and easy access to needs like clean water and cheap housing all stand as potential answers. By tackling these issues, we can create a world in which the rewards and costs of caring for the environment are shared fairly, leading to a more just and sustainable society.

Chapter 7.
Administration and Control

7.1 An overview of international agreements, policies, and regulations related to the environment.

EnvironmentRelated International Treaties, Policies, and Laws: An Overview

Given the scope of environmental problems, nations have banded together to find solutions to shared problems through international agreements. From pollution regulations to biodiversity protection pacts, these policies cover a lot of ground. The role of international environmental agreements in resolving the world's most pressing environmental issues is examined in this overview.

The Urgent Need for Global Environmental Treaties:

All across the world, people are affected by environmental issues. All nations are equally affected by global issues such as air pollution, climate change, biodiversity loss, and the depletion of shared resources like the oceans and the atmosphere. International collaboration and agreements establishing shared goals, standards, and norms are thus necessary for successful response to these difficulties. There are a number of vantage points from which the significance of international environmental agreements can be seen:

1. International Relations The global community is intricately linked. Deforestation and other global warmingrelated phenomena can have farreaching effects on other regions of the planet. These links are acknowledged and addressed in international treaties.

Common Facilities Freshwater supplies, fisheries, and migratory animals are just a few examples of the many natural resources that are shared across international borders. To maintain their longterm viability, international agreements aid in the management and protection of these assets.

Ecological Equality: Vulnerable and marginalised groups are typically hit the hardest by environmental issues. By addressing these inequalities, international accords aim to promote equity and justice.

International accords provide a framework for coordinated action, ensuring that countries adopt uniform approaches to environmental concerns and preventing a race to the bottom in environmental standards.

Important Treaties on the International Environment:

There are a plethora of international organisations and treaties devoted to fixing environmental problems. Here are just a few of the most wellknown and influential:

Convention on Climate Change of the United Nations (UNFCCC):

One of the most wellknown international treaties addressing climate change, the UNFCCC was established in 1992. It lays the groundwork for future climate negotiations and for other related agreements, including the Paris Agreement. To keep global warming below 2 degrees Celsius above preindustrial levels, with an emphasis on keeping it below 1.5 degrees Celsius, the world's nations signed the Paris Agreement in 2015.

Secondly, the CBD (Convention on Biological Diversity):

The Convention on Biological Diversity (CBD) was founded in 1992 as an international accord to protect biodiversity, promote the responsible use of its components, and fairly distribute the benefits gained from the exploitation of genetic resources. Access to genetic resources and the fair and equitable distribution of benefits deriving from their utilisation are the focus of the Nagoya Protocol, established under the CBD in 2010.

Third, substances banned under the Montreal Protocol to Protect the Ozone Layer:

Signed in 1987, the Montreal Protocol is a groundbreaking environmental deal with the goal of protecting Earth's ozone layer by the elimination of ozonedepleting chemicals in production and use. Its efforts have paid off handsomely, as the ozone layer has begun to heal.

The CITES Convention, which regulates the global trade of endangered species of wild animals and plants:

In order to protect endangered species from being overhunted, CITES was founded in 1973 to establish guidelines for international commerce. There are three separate appendices for different types of species, each with its own set of trade and protection regulations.

Fifth, the Basel Convention on the Prevention and Control of Transboundary Movements of Wastes That Contain or Are Designed to Contain Such Wastes:

To prevent hazardous waste from being dumped in poor nations, the Basel Convention was established in 1989 to regulate and restrict its transboundary flow. It deals with the ecologically responsible handling of toxic and other types of garbage.

The Sixth Ramsar Convention on Wetlands of International Significance:

Adopted in 1971, the Ramsar Convention is dedicated to the protection and wise management of the world's wetlands. It promotes the protection of internationally recognised wetland areas.

MARPOL, or the International Convention for the Prevention of Pollution from Ships, is the seventh convention on this list.

Adopted in 1973 and revised in 1978, MARPOL controls oil, chemicals, sewage, and waste discharged from ships. It lays out guidelines and regulations to reduce pollution in the ocean.

The IWC (International Whaling Commission) comes in at number eight:

To safeguard whale populations and maintain their conservation, the IWC created regulations for whaling activities in 1946. The group has instituted limits and moratoriums to limit whaling.

9. The Convention on the World's Heritage Sites:

The World Heritage Convention was established in 1972 to identify and safeguard places of exceptional universal importance to humanity. World Heritage sites are recognised all around the world for their significance.

POPs are persistent organic pollutants, and they're the subject of the Stockholm Convention.

Toxic chemicals that persist in the environment and pose threats to human health were the impetus for the 2001 adoption of the Stockholm Convention to ban or limit their manufacture and use.

Impediments and Constraints:

Despite their importance, international environmental agreements have their limitations when it comes to solving global environmental problems.

Enforcement (No. 1) Many agreements rely on the good faith of their parties and lack effective means for enforcing their terms. Because of this, it might be hard to hold nations responsible for their promises.

2. Difficulty: Complex environmental problems necessitate varied, nuanced solutions.

7.2 The role of governments and organizations in addressing the crisis.

What Governments and NonProfits Can Do to Help

It is the obligation of all parties, including governments, international organisations, NGOs, and others, to work together to solve environmental disasters. These issues, which include climate change, biodiversity loss, pollution, and resource depletion, are so complicated that they can only be addressed effectively by concerted efforts on a regional, national, and international scale. The crucial roles of governments and organisations in responding to environmental disasters are discussed, along with the techniques they have employed, the obstacles they have faced, and the successes they have achieved.

The Function of Government in Solving Environmental Problems:

First, governments develop and enact environmental policies and regulations in order to establish the normative legal framework for dealing with environmental problems. Conservation, pollution prevention, and responsible use of natural resources are all aspects of climate change that are governed by these policies.

Diplomacy and international agreements are two means by which governments attempt to address environmental problems on a global scale. Accords like the Paris Agreement and the Convention on Biological Diversity allow countries to work together to achieve common goals.

Funding and Investment (3) Governments set aside money to ensure the longterm health of the environment. Spending money on study, conservation, renewable energy efforts, and pollution control are all examples.

Lastly, governments do environmental evaluations and monitoring to keep tabs on environmental shifts. These initiatives aid in the detection of new problems, assessment of policy efficacy, and surveillance of adherence to rules.

5. Enforcement of Environmental Laws Governments have a significant responsibility in enforcing environmental laws and holding individuals, corporations, and other entities accountable for noncompliance. Harmful actions towards the environment are deterred by the threat of punishment.

Governments run efforts to raise public awareness of environmental issues and implement educational programmes to teach people how to live more sustainably. They inspire people to adopt practises that promote conservation and longterm viability.

Natural resources such as land, water, and minerals are managed and allocated by governments to ensure their sustainable usage. They lay down rules for the sustainable use of resources and their extraction.

8. Disaster Preparedness and Response: In order to deal with climaterelated occurrences like hurricanes, floods, and wildfires, governments create disaster preparedness plans and response procedures. These precautions are lifesaving and communityaffirming.

Governments may set an example via green procurement regulations, sustainable building standards, and ecofriendly practises in government operations. This serves as an example for the business sector and individual consumers.

Government action: its successes and failures

Governments have an important role in resolving environmental disasters, but they are hampered in their efforts by a number of factors.

(1) Economic and Political Sometimes environmental concerns run counter to political and economic issues. It's possible for policymakers to put shortterm financial benefits ahead of longterm viability.

Second, the lack of international cooperation: Climate change is one worldwide environmental issue that can only be solved by concerted international effort. The implementation of efficient solutions is often slowed down by the length of time it takes to reach an agreement and implement it.

Budget limits: Environmental Protection requires enough funding, yet budgetary limits and competing priorities might reduce the amount of money that is actually spent on environmental protection.

Inconsistent enforcement of environmental rules and regulations might be the consequence of poor leadership, corruption, or a lack of resources, all of which reduce the efficiency of policy.

The Growing Political Divide: Many people in several nations hold radically different views on climate change, conservation, and regulatory measures. Environmental policy advancements may be stymied by this partisanship.

Notable accomplishments have been made by governments despite these obstacles.

1) Eliminating the Use of OzoneDepleting Chemicals: With the help of the international convention known as the Montreal Protocol, many compounds that deplete the ozone layer were banned from usage. The ozone layer is thus showing signs of improvement.

2. Investments in Renewable Energy Renewable energy sources, such as wind and solar, are receiving increased funding from several national governments. The usage of fossil fuels is gradually being phased out, and these projects help with that transition.

Efforts to Conserve 3. Protected areas, marine reserves, and national parks have been established by governments around the world to help preserve wildlife and their natural environments.

4. Efforts to Reduce Pollution and Enhance Air Quality: Many areas now have better air quality thanks to regulations on emissions and pollution control, which has led to lower health risks and a higher quality of life for locals.

5. Reduction Goals for Emissions: The Paris Agreement, ratified by 196 countries, pledges to curb emissions of greenhouse gases and thereby slow the rate at which the planet warms. This historic deal aims high in its pursuit to slow global warming.

The Function of Multinational Agencies:

The efforts of governments are bolstered by those of international organisations, both intergovernmental and nongovernmental, working to alleviate environmental catastrophes. The environmental protection projects are driven by their knowledge, coordination, and advocacy. These are some of the most important worldwide groups:

The United Nations Environment Programme (UNEP) is the specialised agency of the United Nations charged with dealing with environmental concerns. It encourages nations to work together, establishes guidelines for protecting the environment, and backs longterm growth.

The World Wildlife Fund (WWF) is a worldwide organisation (NGO) dedicated to protecting wildlife and their habitats and promoting responsible resource management. It works on conservation projects all across the world and conducts research to better understand our planet.

Third, Greenpeace — Greenpeace is a global environmental organisation that uses directaction campaigns and public campaigning to promote clean energy, chemical safety regulations, and other environmental goals.

4. The Nature Conservancy: This nongovernmental organisation (NGO) aims to preserve ecosystems and biodiversity by protecting land and water. It works with governments and local communities to protect natural resources.

Intergovernmental Panel on Climate Change (IPCC): The IPCC evaluates the science of climate change and its implications, providing policymakers with the data they need to create sensible climate policies.

While its primary focus is on global health, the World Health Organisation (WHO) also has a role to play in environmental health by tackling problems like pollution, disease vectors, and the effects of climate change on public health.

Organisations that are not part of the government:

Nongovernmental organisations (NGOs) are crucial when it comes to promoting sustainability through advocacy, research, and project implementation. To name a few notable environmental NGOs:

(1) The Sierra Club: An influential group in the United States that promotes green power, environmental protection, and climate change solutions.

Second, the Natural Resources Defence Council (NRDC): In order to save our environment and its inhabitants, NRDC engages in legal action, policy advocacy, and public education.

Third, Earth Friends: This coalition of green groups is actively working to combat concerns like global warming, pollution, and the loss of biodiversity.

4. The Rainforest Foundation: This group defends rainforests and the rights of indigenous people who have always called them home.

5. The Environmental Defence Fund: EDF is dedicated to finding answers to environmental problems like pollution in the air and water, global warming, and depleting fish stocks.

Nongovernmental organisations and international challenges and successes:

While making major contributions to resolving environmental disasters, international organisations and NGOs confront their fair share of obstacles.

First, Financial Restrictions: Aid and funding are crucial to the work of many nongovernmental organisations (NGOs) and

Chapter 8.
New Green Technologies and Methods

8.1 Discussion of emerging technologies and innovations to combat environmental issues.

New technologies and innovations for environmental protection are discussed.

Climate change, biodiversity loss, pollution, and resource depletion are just a few environmental concerns that call for creative responses if we are to have any hope of a sustainable future. New inventions and technologies are driving the effort to solve these critical problems. In this article, we'll take a look at some of the most exciting developments in a range of fields that could one day help us solve our environmental problems for good.

1. Technologies that use renewable energy sources:

Reducing greenhouse gas emissions and combating climate change require a shift away from fossil fuels and towards renewable energy. Several cuttingedge technological developments are behind this shift:

Solar Energy The efficiency and cost of solar panels have increased because to developments in photovoltaic technology. Mirror and lensbased concentrated solar power systems are also gaining popularity. In addition, innovative battery technology and other solar energy storage options are facilitating continuous power supply.

Renewable Wind Power: Wind turbines have increased in height and power, making them more efficient. More electricity is being generated as offshore wind farms take advantage of stronger and more persistent winds.

Renewable energy that can be predicted and relied upon, such as that provided by the energy of tides and waves, is currently the focus of research and development.

Energy from Geothermal Sources: Research on improved geothermal systems is being conducted so that the Earth's interior heat can be used. This technology may one day be able to supply reliable, baseload energy.

Fuel cells that run on hydrogen: Interest in hydrogen fuel cells as a means of energy storage and mobility is growing. Hydrogen can be a renewable energy carrier if it is created using clean sources of energy.

2. Sustainable Farming Practises and HighTech Farming:

Food and environmental sustainability depend on agricultural innovations.

Precision Farming: Precision Farming enables more efficient use of water, fertilisers, and pesticides through the use of cuttingedge sensors, drones, and data analytics. The ecological toll of farming is lightened as a result.

Advanced hydroponic and aeroponic technologies are used in vertical farming facilities to cultivate plants in sterile conditions. Reduced water use, fewer pesticides, and yearround harvesting are all benefits of this technique.

Genetic Engineering and CRISPR: Crops with enhanced yields, disease resistance, and lower environmental impact are being developed using genetic engineering techniques such as CRISPR.

Farm photovoltaics Agrivoltaics, the combination of solar energy production and agricultural use, can greatly lessen land and water resource rivalry.

Third, Carbon Utilisation (CCU):

Carbon capture and utilisation technologies are being developed to combat increasing CO2 levels and lessen the effects of climate change.

Direct Atmospheric Capture (DAC) is a technology that removes carbon dioxide (CO2) from the air. This trapped CO2 has multiple potential uses, including but not limited to carbonfree fuel production.

The Process of Mineralization In order to sequester carbon for extended periods of time, several businesses are employing mineralization methods to transform CO2 into stable minerals.

The Use of Carbon Dioxide There are new ways to process CO2 that will yield useful minerals, fuels, and chemicals.

4. Circular Economy Efforts :

The goal of the circular economy is to decrease waste and pollution through increased material and energy conservation as well as recycling and reusing.

New Methods for Reusing Plastic: A circular model for plastic production is encouraged by the fact that plastic waste may be recycled into highquality materials through the use of cuttingedge recycling technology.

New approaches to recycling electronic waste have allowed for the recovery of valuable materials while reducing the load of waste devices sent to landfills.

ClosedLoop Systems: Products that are meant to be easily disassembled and recycled are being investigated as part of closedloop systems for textiles, electronics, and furniture.

5. EcoFriendly Construction and Design:

The way we plan and construct buildings is changing drastically as a result of green building technologies:

The Passive House Standard: Passive home design reduces energy use and carbon dioxide emissions by prioritising highperformance building envelopes, ventilation, and heating systems.

Renewable Resources Greener construction is made possible by the use of cuttingedge sustainable materials such as engineered wood, lowimpact concrete, and highperformance insulation.

Netzero energy buildings use renewable energy sources and energyefficient design to generate as much electricity as they use.

Intelligent Structures: Optimising energy consumption, lighting, and HVAC with the help of building management systems and the internet of things has a positive effect on the environment.

6. Electric and selfdriving cars:

Electric and autonomous vehicles are changing the automobile business.

Electric Vehicles: The price of and availability of EVs are both improving. Increased battery availability and charging infrastructure have the potential to significantly cut transportationrelated greenhouse gas emissions.

Driverless Cars The widespread use of autonomous vehicles has the potential to ease gridlock, streamline commutes, and save costs at the pump. More cars on the road can be avoided with the help of shared autonomous transportation services.

Sustainable Transportation: Efforts like bikesharing, electric scooters, and environmentally responsible forms of public transportation are paving the way for lowimpact and environmentally friendly urban transportation.

7. Solutions Inspired by Nature:

Ecosystems found in nature are used in naturebased solutions to environmental problems.

Restoring the Waterway's Edge Water quality, erosion, and biodiversity can all benefit from protected and restored riparian zones.

Restoration of Forest Cover: Carbon sequestration, wildlife habitat improvement, and soil erosion protection are all benefits of tree planting and forest restoration.

Wetland restoration efforts help with flood mitigation, water purification, and protecting wildlife habitat.

Eighth, Data Analytics and Artificial Intelligence (AI):

The use of AI and data analytics is becoming increasingly important in environmental monitoring and problem solving.

Air quality, deforestation, and wildlife migration are just a few examples of environmental changes that may be monitored and predicted with the use of AIpowered sensors and data analysis.

Modelling the Climate: It is critical for dealing with the effects of climate change that artificial intelligence be utilised to enhance climate modelling and predict catastrophic weather events.

Issues and Things to Think About:

These new technology and developments have a lot of potential, but there are a few things to keep in mind.

1. Deficiencies in Technology There is a global disparity in environmental solutions since not all regions have access to emerging technologies.

Social and Economic Effects Implementation of these technologies should take into account retraining and workforce adaptation in sectors where they may cause job displacement.

8.2 Sustainable practices in agriculture, energy, and transportation.

Sustainable methods in farming, power generation, and driving

As we try to cope with the effects of environmental deterioration, climate change, and resource depletion, the notion of sustainability has risen to prominence in recent years. Sustainable agriculture, energy, and transportation practises are urgently needed as a reaction to these threats. Not only do these industries contribute significantly to environmental problems, but they also provide some of the most promising answers to these problems and pathways towards a more sustainable future. Key sustainable practises in each of these areas, and their effects on environmental, economic, and social wellbeing, will be discussed.

Sustainable farming:

Food, fibre, and jobs for billions of people are all made possible by agriculture, making it an indispensable part of our global society. However, conventional farming techniques frequently have negative effects on the environment, such as the destruction of natural habitats, the contamination of water supplies, and the wasteful use of scarce resources. The goal of sustainable farming methods is to maintain a healthy ecosystem while also meeting human needs for food.

Organic Agriculture Instead of using chemical fertilisers and pesticides, organic farmers turn to timetested techniques like crop rotation, companion planting, and biological pest management. The goal of organic farming is to improve environmental conditions by minimising pollution of soil and water supplies.

The Agroforestry System In agroforestry, trees and bushes are planted in the same area as crops and cattle. By taking all of these measures together, soil fertility is increased, erosion is decreased, carbon is stored, and biodiversity is boosted.

3. Conservation Agriculture: Conservation agriculture employs diversified crop rotations, encourages cover cropping with residue, and reduces the frequency with which soil is disturbed. Soil health, erosion, and carbon sequestration can all be enhanced by adopting these practises.

Precision farming, number four: Precision farming use tools like GPSguided tractors and drones to cut down on wasteful applications of water and fertiliser. This reduces waste and protects natural resources.

The environmental impact of livestock production can be mitigated by the use of sustainable livestock practises such as rotational grazing and the provision of animal welfare.

Agriculture in the City(6) Growing crops and keeping cattle in urban environments is encouraged by advocates of urban agriculture. It can lessen the environmental toll of shipping food large distances.

Seed variety and conventional crops: The preservation of genetic variety and the fortification of resistance against pests and climate change are both aided by encouraging the cultivation of traditional and heirloom crop varieties.

Sustainable Power:

When it comes to protecting the planet, the energy industry is essential because of the impact it has on pollution, resource depletion, and greenhouse gas emissions. Several methods and tools have been created to help us reach the goal of longterm energy sustainability:

1. Natural and Solar Energy Greenhouse gas emissions, air pollution, and resource depletion can all be mitigated by switching from fossil fuels to renewable energy sources like solar, wind, and hydropower.

Buildings, appliances, and industrial operations that use less energy because they are more efficient use less power overall.

Thirdly, Smart Grids allow for more efficient control of electricity distribution, which in turn lessens environmental impact and makes renewable energy sources more feasible to incorporate.

Using renewable electricity to power electric vehicles and home heating systems is a great way to cut down on carbon emissions.

The development of energy storage technology, such as batteries, has made it possible to store renewable energy in excess and use it during times of high demand or low generation.

Carbon capture and storage (CCS) is a technology that removes carbon dioxide from the air by capturing it from sources like factories and power plants and burying it deep underground.

Despite its negative reputation, nuclear power has been defended as a viable option for producing clean power.

Environmentally Friendly Travel:

Greenhouse gas emissions and air pollution are both exacerbated by the transportation sector. The goal of sustainable transportation practises is to lessen these effects without sacrificing convenience or access.

First, Transit Systems: The number of cars on the road can be reduced by investing in effective and widespread public transport networks, which in turn reduces traffic and pollution.

Reduce your dependency on cars and improve your health by encouraging walking and cycling with pedestrianfriendly infrastructure.

Thirdly, Electric Vehicles (EVs): EVs, especially when fuelled by renewable energy, leave behind less carbon than conventional automobiles.

4. HighSpeed Rail: Highspeed rail systems lessen the negative effects of intercity transit on the environment and provide a sustainable alternative to shorthaul air travel.

Sharing rides with others helps cut down on the number of cars on the road and the amount of pollution produced.

Telecommuting and other forms of remote employment help people save money on gas and time by eliminating the need for them to drive to and from work each day.

7. Other Fuels Biofuels, hydrogen, and natural gas are just a few examples of alternative fuels that could be used to lessen transportation's impact on the environment.

Sustainable practises and their effects:

1. Effects on the Environment: Reducing greenhouse gas emissions, conserving resources, and minimising pollution are only some of the direct positive effects of adopting sustainable practises in the agricultural, energy, and transportation sectors. Sustainable farming methods, for instance, lead to cleaner soils, less chemical pollution, and more plant and animal life. The carbon footprint of energy production is greatly reduced when renewable energy sources and energy efficiency measures are used. Cleaner air and less traffic are two of the many benefits of sustainable transportation.

Economic Advantages Taking a more sustainable approach can help you save money and open up business doors. Precision farming and organic farming are two examples of resourceefficient and costeffective agricultural practises. The cost of renewable energy technology has decreased, opening up new markets for investment and the creation of new jobs in the energy industry. Fuelefficient and electric vehicles can help drivers save money on petrol and maintenance.

Thirdly, Social Equity: Promoting food security, access to clean energy, and equitable transportation options are all areas where sustainable practises can have a positive impact on society as a whole. For instance, urban agriculture projects can help those in need gain easier access to healthy foods. Renewable energy projects have the potential to improve energy access in rural areas while also creating new jobs. Sustainable modes of transport help to level the playing field by providing accessible and costeffective mobility alternatives.

(4) Resilience and Adaptability: Resilience to climate change and other environmental stresses can be boosted through sustainability practises.

Chapter 9.
The Role of the Individual and the Group

9.1 Empowering individuals to make environmentally conscious choices.

Facilitating Individual Decisions That Are Better for the Environment

Climate change, biodiversity loss, and pollution are just a few examples of the environmental crises that call for not just systemic but also human action. Our collective decisions as customers, citizens, and members of communities have farreaching effects on Earth. One of the most important goals of the sustainability movement is to encourage human action that is environmentally responsible. The relevance of people's own initiatives and plans to motivate and equip them to live more sustainably will be discussed.

The Influence of Free Will:

The world we live in is shaped by the decisions of individuals. While institutional shifts are essential, we should not discount the power of a billion people making deliberate decisions. Here are several ways in which one person can help the planet:

Carbon emissions, a major contributor to climate change, can be reduced by measures such as decreasing vehicle use, increasing the efficiency of household appliances, and switching to renewable energy sources.

Reducing, reusing, and recycling are all actions that may be taken by individuals to help preserve our finite supply of resources and cut down on unnecessary garbage.

3. Supporting Sustainable Practises: Individuals may urge businesses to embrace more sustainable practises by purchasing sustainable items like organic foods, sustainably sourced commodities, and ecofriendly materials.

Protecting and restoring natural ecosystems is one way that people may work to maintain biodiversity.

5. Reducing Pollution: Pollution and its detrimental effects on ecosystems can be mitigated by the responsible use and disposal of chemicals, plastics, and garbage.

6. Inspiring and Educating Others: One person's efforts might have a domino impact on the environmental awareness of others.

Individual Obstacles and Difficulties:

Although people have a lot of ability to make decisions, there are a number of obstacles that can prevent them from becoming environmentally conscious:

1. Inattention Many people probably don't know how their actions affect the planet or what other options they have.

2. Inertia: People are notoriously bad at breaking out of their ruts and embracing novel, longterm patterns of behaviour.

Thirdly, Financial Constraints: Some people with lesser salaries may feel that sustainable solutions are out of their price range.

The Ease of It All Some people are dissuaded from making sustainable decisions because they are inconvenient or timeconsuming.

5. Common Practises The way people act might be influenced by the expectations of others. If people believe they will be stigmatised for making environmentally friendly decisions, they may think twice before making those decisions.

Individual Empowerment Strategies:

Several methods can be used to overcome these obstacles and encourage people to make ecologically responsible decisions:

First, Awareness and Education:

   Educate people regarding environmental problems, their origins, and the effects of doing nothing. Encourage people to think about the environmental effects of their behaviour.

   Make data about ecofriendly lifestyles readily available. These materials cover topics including sustainable energy, trash management, and shopping.

2. Nudges (or Nudging):

   Promoting sustainable actions through the application of behavioural science principles. Increasing the rate of adoption, for instance, is possible by making ecofriendly choices the default.

   Use social pressure and group beliefs to inspire people to take action. When people see that others are making ecofriendly decisions, it can motivate them to do the same.

Financial Incentives 3.

   Create monetary incentives that praise ecofriendly actions. Tax credits for utilising public transit, rebates for buying energyefficient appliances, and so on all fall under this category.

Internalise the environmental costs of carbon emissions through carbon pricing mechanisms like carbon taxes or capandtrade systems to motivate individual and corporate carbon reduction.

4. Requirements and Guidelines

Sustainability standards for goods and services can be set by governments and regulated by authorities. Labelling initiatives (such as Energy Star and Fair Trade) direct shoppers towards more ecofriendly products.

Restrict or eliminate environmentally damaging practises and substances, such as singleuse plastics or highly polluting materials, by the implementation of policy.

Participation in the Community 5.

Encourage communityled efforts that unite neighbours in taking on environmental issues. A sense of community can be fostered through the cultivation of communal gardens, the organisation of neighbourhood cleanups, and the installation of renewable energy systems.

Help out community groups and environmental groups doing good work in your area. When backed by wider networks, grassroots initiatives can make a far bigger difference.

Sixthly, Affordability and Access:

Make an effort to reduce the high cost of going green. Clean energy technologies, public transport, and sustainable food can all benefit from increased accessibility thanks to government subsidies or grants.

Prompt companies to use ecofriendly procedures and supply customers with cheaper green products.

7. Innovation and Technology:

Take advantage of modern tools to simplify and expedite the process of making ecofriendly decisions. Home automation technology, for instance, can help reduce energy consumption, while transportation apps for smartphones can detail bus routes and carpooling opportunities.

Sustainable product and material innovations provide people preferable substitutes to conventional, ecologically damaging products and materials.

8. Schooling and Skill Development:

Encourage learning and skill development concerning sustainable practises. This involves instructing people on how to start their own gardens, fix broken goods, and minimise trash.

Maintain funding for community and schoolbased environmental education programmes.

Studies of Individual Empowerment:

Waste Reduction and Recycling Programmes

Recycling and trash reduction programmes have been launched in many communities, with the goals of raising awareness about the necessity of recycling and making curbside recycling pickup more accessible. Rates of recycling have increased dramatically as a result of these initiatives.

(2) Incentives for Electric Vehicles:

Tax credits, rebates, and priority in carpool lanes are just some of the incentives that governments throughout the world offer to drivers of electric vehicles. As a result of these incentives, the number of electric vehicles on the road has increased, and the transportation sector's contribution to greenhouse gas emissions has decreased.

3. Labelling for Energy Efficiency

Labels, such as Energy Star's, that indicate a product's energy efficiency are helpful for shoppers. With the help of these labels, consumers can make more ecofriendly purchases that are better for the environment and their wallets.

Conclusion:

An integral part of our joint efforts to solve environmental concerns is enabling individuals to make ecologically conscientious decisions. It's apparent that people's activities add up, even if institutional shifts and policy decisions play a significant effect.

9.2 The importance of community engagement and global cooperation.

The Value of Local Involvement and International Collaboration

It will take more than individual efforts or government initiatives to solve the world's environmental problems. To achieve this goal, people on a global scale must work together with those in their own communities. Sustainable development requires people all around the world to work together for the common good. The relevance of these two factors in the larger movement to protect our environment is explored.

Engaging Communities for Local Resilience and Accountability

The term "community engagement" is used to describe when individuals, groups, and businesses in a certain area work together to find solutions to environmental problems. Among its many important contributions to environmental sustainability are the following:

Local Expertise and Creative Answers Communities have unique insights on their ecosystems, natural resources, and environmental challenges. This information is crucial for developing tailored responses and flexible plans.

Responsibility and ownership 2 Communities benefit emotionally and intellectually when members take part in environmental activities. This responsibility guarantees that local resources are managed effectively and that laws are followed.

3. Constructing Resilience The effects of natural disasters, such as floods, droughts, or wildfires, can be felt very immediately in affected communities. Their capacity to endure and recover from such calamities can be improved through participation in preparedness and resiliencebuilding programmes.

Social cohesiveness and communal togetherness are two outcomes of environmental projects. Volunteering for a common cause, like treeplanting or litterpicking, can bring people closer together.

5. Behaviour Change: Localised campaigns of environmental education and awareness can inspire people to make positive changes in their daily routines, such as recycling more often, practising sustainable agriculture, and minimising their use of natural resources.

Local Efforts, No. 6 Local environmental projects like community gardens, garbage recycling programmes, and green energy cooperatives typically sprout from active citizenry. These actions aid in the larger fight for environmental preservation.

CommunityDriven Reforestation in Kenya: A Case Study

An outstanding example of community involvement in environmental protection is the Green Belt Movement in Kenya, which was started by Nobel Peace Prize winner Wangari Maathai. The initiative encourages people, especially women, to reforest their communities and revitalise damaged environments. They have helped with reforestation, watershed protection, and the reduction of soil erosion by planting approximately 51 million trees.

International Coordination: Tackle Global Problems

Community involvement looks for answers close to home, yet environmental problems with transnational and universal consequences require international collaboration to solve. The following details highlight why international cooperation is crucial for environmental sustainability:

First, International Concerns: Air and water pollution, biodiversity loss, and climate change are just few of the environmental concerns that know no boundaries. Coordinated international effort is often necessary to achieve lasting solutions.

Common Facilities When addressing issues involving transboundary rivers, fisheries, and the atmosphere, international cooperation is crucial. Treaties and agreements aid in the administration and protection of these assets.

3. Adaptation to Climate Change Reducing greenhouse gas emissions and preparing for the effects of climate change requires concerted action on a global scale. The global effort to tackle climate change is exemplified by the Paris Agreement, which was signed by practically every government in the world.

The Protection of Biological Diversity The world's biodiversity is a shared resource that must be safeguarded together. Global biodiversity protection and sustainable use are promoted by the Convention on Biological Diversity.

Management of Resources: International agreements are often necessary to prevent overexploitation and resource conflicts associated with the responsible management of natural resources like minerals and forests.

Collaboration between nations facilitates the exchange of information, resources, and expertise that improves everyone's ability to deal with environmental issues.

The Montreal Protocol for Substances that Deplete the Ozone Layer as a Case Study

One of the best examples of successful international cooperation is the Montreal Protocol. This worldwide agreement was signed in 1987 with the goal of protecting Earth's ozone layer by reducing or eliminating the use of substances that deplete it. The ozone layer has recovered thanks to the treaty's efforts, and dangerous UV radiation is now again unable to reach Earth's surface.

Interactions between Local Action and International Partnerships:

Volunteering and international cooperation are not alternatives but complements to one another. Communities on a smaller scale are often essential in influencing international treaties and agreements. See how they overlap below:

1. Global Negotiations with Local Input The global negotiations can be aided by the local experiences and views. Traditional knowledge regarding how to manage resources in a sustainable way is something that is often held by indigenous cultures.

2. Implementation of Policy The local level is frequently the best place for international agreements to be put into effect. Conservation of biodiversity and cutting down on carbon emissions are only two examples of environmental protection measures that rely heavily on the participation of local communities.

3. Innovation and Grassroots activities: Efforts started at the local level can have a profound impact on activities on a global scale. Sustainable practises often emerge from grassroots initiatives and go on to influence bigger policy shifts.

Fourthly, "Solidarity" and "Advocate": Environmental causes can benefit from the worldwide advocacy of local communities. They can strengthen their collective voice by joining forces with networks and organisations on a global scale.

5. Research and Data Collection: Local Community Contributions to Environmental Studies. This data is crucial for determining where we

stand environmentally, establishing worldwide goals, and tracking our development.

Environmental Education: Local education and awareness initiatives can generate a worldwide understanding of environmental challenges and a call to action.

Barriers and Obstacles to International Cooperation:

Although global collaboration is crucial, it confronts several obstacles.

First, Differing Interests: Countries' priorities may be at odds with one another, especially when it comes to the distribution of scarce resources or the promotion of prosperous economies. This creates a delicate balancing act in international discussions.

2. No Mechanisms for Enforcing Compliance Without effective enforcement measures, it can be difficult to hold countries to account for violations of international agreements.

Economic and Political Pressures, 3. In international discussions, environmental concerns are sometimes overshadowed by political and commercial objectives.

Inequalities in global collaboration can be exacerbated by differences in economic resources and development levels. It may be difficult for developing nations to contribute meaningfully to international initiatives.

5. Concerns About Sovereignty Worries about encroaching on national sovereignty by other countries might make international agreements difficult to implement.

Chapter 10.
Prospects for LongTerm Sustainability

10.1 A call to action and a vision for a sustainable future.

A Plea for Change and a Plan for the Future

Urgent and interconnected, the threats to our world today range from climate change and environmental deterioration to resource depletion and the loss of species. There must be immediate and extensive action to solve these problems. Present and future generations' happiness depends on our ability to create a sustainable future. This conversation is a rallying cry; it highlights the significance of joint efforts and lays out a desirable future in which we can live sustainably.

The Immediate Plea

First, Actions to Reduce Global Warming The risk of climate change is among the most pressing global challenges we face today. Reducing greenhouse gas emissions, shifting to renewable energy, and adjusting to the changes that are already here are all urgently needed. We need fast and coordinated action from governments, businesses, and individuals to fix this.

Conserving Biodiversity The fast deterioration of biodiversity endangers both ecosystems and human life. Deforestation, habitat loss, and overexploitation are all contributors to this problem that need to be addressed alongside protecting natural habitats and adopting sustainable landuse practises.

Thirdly, Resource Efficiency: Depleting the Earth's finite resources due to excessive consumption. For optimal use of available resources, it is necessary to adopt circular economy concepts, prioritise recycling, and cut down on waste production.

Ecosystems and human health are negatively impacted by pollution from a variety of sources, such as factories, farms, and plastics. To combat pollution, society must embrace cleaner technologies, decrease reliance on chemicals, and encourage ethical garbage disposal.

Constructing Resilience 5. In order to better deal with environmental threats, our society must become more robust. Among these measures are bolstering infrastructure so that it can resist extreme weather, funding agriculture that can withstand changing temperatures, and encouraging community resilience.

Transforming the agricultural industry to incorporate sustainable practises is crucial, which brings us to point number six: Sustainable Agriculture. This includes embracing practises like organic farming, agroforestry, and precision farming.

Environmentally Friendly City Planning: As more people move into cities, sustainable urban planning is more important than ever. For this reason, it is important to improve public transit, provide access to parks, and lessen the negative environmental impacts of cities.

Eighth, Environmental Instruction: Change can only be prompted by increased environmental literacy. Curriculum reform is needed to include environmental education, increase public consciousness, and advance scientific knowledge of the natural world.

A LongTerm Plan for Sustainability:

We can move towards a sustainable future by making responsible decisions and taking action in the here and now. Several crucial elements make up a future that is sustainable:

One World Prepared for Climate Change: In this scenario, drastic measures to reduce emissions of greenhouse gases have successfully averted climate change's most severe effects. Carbonneutral technologies are the norm, and the shift to renewable energy sources is complete. This has led to a levelling out of global temperatures and a decrease in the frequency of extreme weather occurrences. The remaining climate problems are better able to be weathered by ecosystems and communities.

Biodiversity that Thrives In a sustainable future, all forms of life are respected and protected. There has been an increase in marine and terrestrial reserves. The successful recovery of oncethreatened species is a direct result of the adoption of sustainable landuse practises. The planet's biological diversity is safe from the effects of human activities.

3. Effective Use of Resources: The world economy has been revolutionised by improved resource efficiency. The circular economy is a comprehensive strategy for minimising waste and maximising product durability. Materials are frequently recycled and used to reduce waste and conserve supplies. Sustainable practises have become the norm, therefore resource disputes are uncommon.

Spotless and wholesome settings, number four The use of ecofriendly tools and ethical behaviour has considerably cut down on pollution. We now have cleaner air and water, and less dangerous substitutes for oncecommon hazardous substances. The plastic pollution problem has been solved, and the oceans no longer contain garbage islands made entirely of plastic.

5] Resilient Food Systems: Healthy, locally sourced food is the norm, thanks to the prevalence of sustainable agriculture. Agroforestry and organic farming are two methods that improve soil quality, water availability, and agricultural biodiversity. Reduced food waste and increased food security for a growing global population.

Sustainable and EcoFriendly Urban Areas: The urban landscape has been improved by adding greenery and other amenities. In terms of congestion and pollution, public transport systems are highly effective and easily accessible. Urban dwellers benefit from cleaner air and a stronger connection to nature thanks to the city's parks and other green infrastructure.

7. Empowering People Through Environmental Education A key component of a future that can be sustained is quality education. An appreciation for nature is fostered through the incorporation of environmental literacy into curricula at all grade levels. People have the freedom to make ecologically responsible decisions and get involved in local projects.

Just and fair societies, No. 8. The pursuit of ecological sustainability is guided by principles of equity. Communities at risk are safeguarded from environmental hazards and given access to sustainable practises. Sustainable development helps everyone and helps narrow the economic gap.

Countries work together to solve environmental problems that affect multiple countries. All relevant international treaties and agreements are respected, enforced, and regularly revised to address new threats. There is a pervasive awareness of one's role in ensuring the survival of our world.

The Way Forward: Transforming Ideas into Actions

Together with one another, we can make this sustainable future a reality. That means:

Governments must enact and implement regulations that encourage sustainability, punish bad practises, and hasten the use of renewable energy.

2. Innovation in Business Green technologies, sustainable practises, and corporate social responsibility are all areas in which the private sector may make a significant impact.

Participation in the Community: Communities need to take responsibility for environmental issues by getting involved in conservation, patronising green businesses, and lobbying for positive change in their area.

Environmental education programmes and awareness campaigns are crucial to influencing behaviour and generating motivation for change.

When dealing with transboundary problems like climate change, pollution, and resource management, international cooperation is essential.

Individual Accountability: Every individual can do their part for the environment by lowering their carbon footprint, purchasing sustainable goods, and participating in local activities.

Conclusion:
Together, we can work towards a sustainable future, which is not some unreachable ideal. Resolving environmental problems and making the globe a safer place for future generations calls for immediate action. In order to create a world in which human and environmental wellbeing are equally prioritised, it is necessary to embrace the vision of a sustainable future. This better, more sustainable future is within our reach if we all pitch in.

10.2 Steps individuals, governments, and organizations can take to mitigate the crisis.

Ways in Which Communities, Nations, and Corporations Can Respond to the Emerging Emergency

Climate change, biodiversity loss, pollution, and resource depletion are just some of the environmental concerns we face as a planet, and they call for a comprehensive response from individuals, governments, and organisations. Collective effort, shared accountability, and concrete actions are required to lessen the severity of these disasters. The exact actions that each of these groups can take to promote environmental sustainability will be explored in this article.

Personal Initiatives:

Reducing one's carbon footprint is as simple as cutting back on energy use, purchasing energyefficient appliances, taking public transit, walking, biking, or carpooling, and advocating for the use of renewable energy.

Second, Conserving Energy: Saving money on utility bills is as simple as switching off lights, devices, and appliances when they are not in use, installing insulation, and using less heat and air conditioning.

Waste Prevention 3. Recycle, compost, and use less singleuse plastic to cut down on garbage. Buy in bulk and select items with little packaging to lessen your environmental impact.

Transition to a more sustainable diet by eating less meat, more plants, and supporting local and organic farmers. 4. Sustainable Diet.

5. Ethical Purchasing Always do your research before making a purchase. Choosing products with ecolabels and favouring longlasting, durable goods can help you decrease waste while also supporting businesses that care about the environment.

Fixing leaks, installing waterefficient equipment, and being conscientious about water use in daily life all contribute to a lower water bill and a healthier environment.

Keeping pesticides and herbicides out of your garden and encouraging the use of native plant species are great ways to preserve biodiversity.

Join a group working to improve the environment, help out with conservation and cleanup projects in your community, and lobby for greener laws and regulations.

Environmentalism in the Classroom: No. 9 Spread environmental awareness through learning and discussion. Learn about and spread the latest information about conservation and sustainability efforts.

Reduce, reuse, and recycle 10 The adage "reduce, reuse, and recycle" is a potent instrument for lowering garbage output and improving environmental sustainability. Instead of using disposable items, switch to products that can be reused or recycled.

Laws and Regulations

First, Policies to Reduce Emissions: Greenhouse gas emission reduction policies should be implemented and strictly enforced by governments. Carbon pricing schemes, such as carbon taxes or capandtrade systems, may be implemented alongside targets for lowering emissions and increasing use of clean energy.

Second, invest in renewable energy sources like wind, solar, and hydroelectric power to lessen our dependency on fossil fuels and hasten the adoption of more sustainable technologies.

Reduce industrial pollution and save natural ecosystems by strictly enforcing environmental restrictions. Standards for water quality, limitations on pollutants, and protections for endangered species should all be enshrined in law.

Protected areas, such as national parks and wildlife sanctuaries, should be established and kept in good condition if they are to serve their intended purpose of preserving natural resources and promoting animal and plant life for future generations.

5. Incentives for Sustainable Agriculture Incentives should be offered to farmers that adopt environmentally friendly methods like agroforestry and organic farming. If you want to help the environment, it's important to back smallscale and local farms.

Invest on public transportation, make streets safer for pedestrians and cyclists, and encourage people to drive electric and fuelefficient cars.

Seventh, Environmental Education: Incorporate environmental education into K12 curricula and raise public understanding about the importance of sustainability.

International Treaties 8. Take part in international treaties and pacts meant to solve environmental issues on a global scale. Follow through on pledges to the Convention on Biological Diversity and the Paris Agreement to slow climate change.

Programmes for Waste Management Create systems to handle trash that take into account recycling, composting, and proper disposal. Encourage a circular economy and establish waste reduction goals.

Funding for Research and Development (R&D) 10: Invest in green tech R&D to find solutions to the world's environmental problems.

Measures Taken by the Organisation

Supply Chain Sustainability: 1. In order to reduce their environmental impact, businesses should evaluate and improve their supply chains, giving preference to vendors who employ ecofriendly procedures and promote responsible purchasing.

(2) Energy Efficiency: Upgrade to more energyefficient lighting, HVAC, and other systems throughout the company.

Thirdly, Carbon Neutrality: Strive towards carbon neutrality by cutting emissions inhouse and funding carbon offset projects like treeplanting and renewable energy generation.

4. Waste Reduction: Establish recycling and papersaving programmes throughout the company and encourage employees to use reusable materials whenever possible.

Green building refers to the practise of constructing or renovating a structure in a way that minimises its impact on the environment.

To demonstrate environmental effect, progress towards sustainability goals, and operational transparency, businesses should issue yearly sustainability reports.

To create and advocate for ecofriendly goods and services, see the section on "Green Product Development" below. Put your items' sustainability on display by utilising ecolabels.

Worker Involvement, No. 8 Involve workers in environmental preservation initiatives. Workplaces should actively promote energy and waste reduction and give workers opportunity to participate in environmental activities.

9. Invest in Sustainability: Commit funds to ecofriendly projects and innovations including renewable energy, trash reduction, and sustainable study and development.

Tenth, involve your stakeholders (clients, vendors, and environmental groups) in the process of creating and implementing sustainable policies and procedures.

Actions Taken in Collaboration:

1. PPPs (or "publicprivate partnerships"). Encourage public and private sector cooperation in solving environmental problems. Businesses and governments can work together to encourage environmentally responsible practises.

Chapter 11.
The Need for Rapid Alteration

11.1 Summarizing key points and emphasizing the urgency of addressing the global environmental crisis.

An Overview of the Global Environmental Crisis and the Immediacy of Doing Something About It

There are several facets to the current environmental catastrophe that need to be addressed immediately by individuals, governments, organisations, and societies as a whole. In this allencompassing analysis, we have covered: historical background; the development of environmental consciousness; climate change; the results of increased temperatures and melting ice; the plight of endangered species; pollution; the depletion of natural resources; the feasibility of viable sustainable alternatives; the impact on marginalised communities; international agreements; the function of global governance; and, finally, the role of government. Let us briefly review this material and stress the essential importance of acting quickly to resolve the worldwide environmental problem.

Evolution of Environmental Consciousness and Its Historical Context:

The first step in our quest was learning about the background that shaped modern environmental activism. Humanity's impact on Earth has been widely acknowledged, beginning with the Industrial Revolution and continuing into the present day with the Environmental Movement. Because of rising levels of environmental consciousness, policies, rules, and international accords have been established to help ease environmental problems.

Implications of Climate Change:

Greenhouse gas emissions have contributed to one of the world's most critical problems: climate change. It has dire repercussions, such as increased global temperatures, more frequent and intense extreme weather events, rising sea levels, and ecosystem changes. Swift and transformative action is needed to transition to renewable energy sources, reduce emissions, and adapt to the changes that are currently occurring if we are to successfully mitigate climate change.

Studies of the Impacts of Increasing Temperatures and the Retreating Ice Cap:

Increases in the frequency and severity of storms, droughts, and wildfires are some of the environmental repercussions of climate change. Temperature increases are harmful to ecosystems, economy, and people. Rising sea levels, caused in part by melting ice caps and glaciers, threaten coastal and lowlying areas.

The Consequences of Biodiversity Loss

One of the most serious consequences of the environmental disaster is the extinction of oncethriving species. Loss of biodiversity has farreaching effects, affecting everything from food webs to disease resistance to the availability of therapeutic and agricultural materials. The planet's resilience to environmental change is also threatened by the loss of biodiversity.

Species and ecosystems that are at danger of extinction have profiles here.

Human actions such as deforestation, overfishing, and habitat degradation are threatening the survival of many species and ecosystems. African elephants, Bengal tigers, and coral reefs are just few of the endangered species whose suffering highlights the urgent need for conservation efforts to safeguard these critical components of our planet's biodiversity.

Examining the Effects of Environmental Pollution on Human Health (Air, Water, and Soil):

Air, water, and soil pollution all have serious consequences for ecosystems and human health. Pollutants in the air cause respiratory illnesses, in the water they pollute our drinking supply, and in the soil they destroy our ability to grow food. Reducing pollution is essential for preserving ecosystems and people's health.

Impact of Manufacturing, Farming, and Transportation on Environmental Quality:

Pollution has major contributors in the industrial, agricultural, and transportation sectors. Degradation of the natural world is hastened by activities such as manufacturing's emissions, farming's chemical runoff, and transportation's usage of fossil fuels. Mitigating these problems requires a shift to more environmentally friendly technologies and methods.

The Dangers of Exhausting Our Natural Resources

The depletion of the Earth's limited resources is a direct result of the irresponsible and excessive use of its natural assets. The lifespan of these critical resources depends on the implementation of good management practises, the reduction of waste, and the promotion of conservation.

Sustainable Options and the Value of Conserving Resources:

The answer to solving the environmental disaster is to encourage sustainability and resource conservation. Organic farming, renewable energy sources, and efficient public transit are all examples of environmentally friendly agricultural, energy, and transportation practises. Taking up these alternate methods contributes to a greener and more sustainable future.

Analysis of the Intersection of Environmental, Social, and Economic Factors:

Social and economic issues have profound effects on environmental problems. Food security, water availability, and livelihoods are all put at risk by climate change, pollution, and resource depletion, all of which exacerbate preexisting disparities. It will take a holistic strategy, taking into account both social and economic factors, to overcome these obstacles.

The Effects on Socially Weakened Groups and Possible Responses:

Communities already on the margins of society are frequently hit the hardest by environmental problems. Pollution, climate change, and depletion of resources have the greatest impact on them. The only way to reduce environmental inequalities is to empower these communities, give them access to clean resources, and adopt fair regulations.

Environmentrelated international treaties, policies, and regulations:

In order to effectively handle global environmental issues, international agreements and laws are essential. International attempts to prevent climate change, safeguard biodiversity, and decrease ozonedepleting compounds include the Paris Agreement, the Convention on Biological Diversity, and the Montreal Protocol.

Government and NonGovernmental Organisations' Part in Resolving the Crisis:

Policies and measures to address the environmental problem must be implemented by governments and other organisations. They need to incentivize green behaviour by investing in green technology and innovation and by strictly enforcing environmental laws.

New technologies and innovations for environmental protection are discussed.

New technologies, such as renewable energy, carbon capture and storage, and environmentally responsible farming methods, are crucial in solving environmental problems. There is hope that technological advances in these areas will help us curb emissions, preserve resources, and slow the rate of climate change.

Agriculture, energy, and transportation sustainability:

Sustainability in farming, power generation, and transportation is crucial for mitigating negative effects on the natural world. Developing sustainable practises such as agroforestry, using renewable energy sources, and expanding public transportation networks are crucial steps towards creating a better society.

The Value of Local Involvement and International Cooperation:

To solve the environmental catastrophe, people all around the world need to work together.

11.2 Encouraging readers to become informed and take action.

Motivating Audiences to Learn More and Act

Every person must do their part to create a sustainable future in the face of the global environmental disaster. Educating yourself and taking part in the process are not merely desirable, but necessary steps. All of the problems we've discussed so far—from global warming to pollution to the extinction of species—are critical and intertwined. We need to educate ourselves, raise public consciousness, and take part in constructive solutions. In this final section, we will examine ways in which you can put your newfound knowledge into practise. Let's dive into the why, how, and what of its critical importance.

The Critical Need to Act Now:

The environmental problems we have to solve are getting worse, and fast. Communities and ecosystems are already feeling the effects of climate change, from increased frequency and intensity of heat waves to rising sea levels. The ongoing decline of biodiversity poses a serious risk to the wellbeing and stability of our planet. Both human health and environmental health are being threatened by pollution and resource depletion.

Protecting our way of life is equally as important as keeping a clean natural environment. Food security and public health are also threatened by climate change. The deterioration of air and water quality due to pollution has realworld consequences. Ecosystems that provide vital functions like pollination and water purification are threatened when biodiversity is lost.

We owe it to ourselves and to the next generation to find solutions to these problems as responsible global citizens. If we wait too long to take action, the problem will only get worse. Now is the time for serious action.

Acquiring Knowledge:

One must arm oneself with knowledge before taking effective action. In order to educate oneself about environmental issues, consider the following.

First, Keep Up to Date: Stay uptodate on environmental news by subscribing to reputable news outlets, websites, and social media profiles. This will allow you to keep up with current events and scientific inquiry.

2. Research Books and Reports: Dig into writings from scientists and environmentalists. They offer insightful analysis and commentary on numerous facets of the ecological situation.

Third, Read Academic Journals Academic journals publish a plethora of research studies investigating environmental concerns. If you want to learn more about the scientific aspects, you can find these resources online or in your local library.

View Documentaries 4 The problems facing the environment and possible remedies are the subject of numerous documentaries. They frequently weave fascinating tales into informative scientific studies.

5. Join Environmental Organisations: Think about joining or volunteering with an organisation that works to protect the environment. Resources, news, and reading materials are common offerings.

Take Part in Online Communities and Forums Dedicated to Environmental Concerns. You can learn a lot from other people, ask questions, and share what you know in these settings.

7. Enrol in Virtual Classrooms: There is a wealth of low or nocost online environmental studies courses available from a variety of institutions and websites. The breadth of topics covered in these classes is extensive, from climate science to environmental protection.

8. Participate in Regional Meetings and Conferences: Workshops, seminars, and other events on environmental subjects are frequently held by local organisations and educational institutions. These events can be great for making connections and gaining new knowledge.

The Next Steps:

Learning the facts is the starting point, but it's not enough on its own. Here are some tangible things you can do:

1. Lessen Your Footprint On The Environment Reduce your impact on the environment by modifying your habits. Reduce your car use, increase your plantbased diet, and back renewable energy sources to help the environment.

Fix any leaks you find, invest in waterefficient equipment, and be conscious of how much water you use every day to bring your total use down.

Thirdly, recycle, compost, and minimise your usage of singleuse plastics at home to help the environment and save money. Pick out items that don't come with a lot of packing.

Encourage EcoFriendly Enterprises Pick to spend your money with companies who care about the environment. Do your research and give preference to businesses who have solid environmental policies and practises.

Advocate for Alteration 5: Participate actively in campaigns for environmental legislation on the state, federal, and international levels. Take an active role in environmental causes, communicate with your elected officials, and use your voice to advocate for change.

The sixth item on the list is to "Support Conservation Efforts:" donate to and volunteer for environmental groups. Cleanups, wildlife surveys, and the maintenance of natural areas are all examples.

7. Teach and Motivate Others Tell your loved ones and neighbours about the environmental problems you're working to solve. Action can be motivated by education.

8. Join Restoration Projects: Take part in initiatives designed to revitalise and preserve natural habitats. Projects like tree planting, restoring wetlands, and fixing up coral reefs fall within this category.

Participate in Sustainable Agriculture: Back ecofriendly farming methods in your area. Support local farmers by shopping from them directly, joining CSAs, and opting for organics whenever possible.

Ten. Lessen Your Impact on the Environment: Think about your impact on the environment and try to cut back where you can. This entails such practises as recycling, reusing, and cutting back where possible.

11. Think Before You Vote Vote for politicians who will champion environmental protections and make them a priority in government.

Investing responsibly means thinking about investments that benefit society and the environment in equal measure.

Collective Action and Its Potential:

Collective action has a greater influence than the sum of its parts. People's ability to affect change at the governmental, corporate, and community levels increases when they band together. The Clean Air Act and the Paris Agreement are just two of the landmark achievements made possible by people working together.

Participating in local environmental organisations or taking part in global climate marches are both examples of collective action. Your influence can be magnified by forming alliances with other people who share your goals and working together on projects.

Youth's Crucial Part:

The youth generation has been instrumental in bringing about positive environmental change. A new generation of climate activists, inspired by leaders like Greta